THE LIBERATION OF THE LAITY

The scope and gravity of the process of liberation is such that to ponder its significance is really to examine the meaning of Christianity itself and the mission of the Church in the world.

—Gustavo Gutiérrez,
A Theology of Liberation

THE LIBERATION OF THE LAITY

Anne Rowthorn

MOREHOUSE PUBLISHING
Harrisburg, PA / Wilton, CT

Morehouse Publishing

Editorial Office
78 Danbury Road
Wilton, CT 06897

Corporate Office
P.O. Box 1321
Harrisburg, PA 17105

Library of Congress Cataloging-in-Publication Data

Rowthorn, Anne W.
The liberation of the laity.

Bibliography; p.
Includes index.
I. Laity. I. Title.
BV687.R68 1986 262'.15 86-17982
ISBN 0-8192-1395-0

Printed in the United States of America

2 4 6 8 10 9 7 5 3

Second Printing, 1990

DEDICATION

This book is dedicated to all the lay saints, past and present, ordinary and extraordinary, famous and infamous and obscure—lay saints whose holy living, or being, or music, or courageous political leadership, or writings, or witness, or art have formed the life of the world and the Church and, in particular, the life of this writer. A few of them are:

Dag Hammarskjöld, Charles Lawrence, Nancy Lambert, Dorothy Day, Abraham Lincoln, Theodora Glover, Nannie P. Rogers, Cesar Chavez, Mollie Witcomb, Ada Eden, Easter Charman, Thomas Charman, Alene M. Tate, Ernest Williams, Jill Bigwood, Lloyd Coldwell, Constance J. Shrigley, Beatrice Dodge, John F. Kennedy, Eileen Trower, Sidney Trower, Hamish MacEwan, John Mogabgab, Prisca Cull, Kenyon Cull, Evelyn Two Hawk, John Steinbeck, James DiMeo, Eleanor Roosevelt, Ransey Cole, Edith Ball, Eunice Miller, Isaac Hawk, Gertrude Jackson, Esther Burgess, Ilse Fuller, Barbara Coulombe, Joan Bray, Mohandas Gandhi, Jacob Epstein, Anwar Sadat, Enid Dillistone, Judy Conley, Elisabeth S. Bundy, Howard Wheeler, Virginia Mary Rowthorn, Christian Rowthorn, Peregrine Alban Jeffery Rowthorn, Nancy W. Speed, Virginia S. Almy, John Hearne, Thomas Hooker, Raymond Esposito, David Watts, George McGovern, Jane Hooker, Michael Pointer, Patricia Maynard, Suzanne Abrams, Marg Van Cleef, Georgia Knoble, E. Laird Mortimer, Jacob Riis, Granville Sharp, Bruce Fox, Florence Nightingale, George Murdoch, George R. Smith, Eldridge Cleaver, James Baldwin, Toby Turner, Connie Annand, Suzie Wojewoda, Cora Cobey, Gladys Druce, June Eden, Maria Woodward, Elsie Flood, Howard Wheeler III, Sally Palmer, George Cunningham, Edna Carnegie, Hugh Sutherland, Laura Deming, Carole Whiteside, Anne Bennett, Clare Davis, John H. Wheeler, Jay Wheeler, Louisa Turner, Minot B. Nettleton, Peter Waldo, Ruth Carter, Alice Ruotolo, Phillips H. Lovering, Ernest S. Dodge, Sharon Richardson, C. Wright Mills, Robert Frost, Jorge H. Lee, William Rambo, Ned Bayne, Courtney B. Bourns, Harry Puddyfoot, Robert Gray, Eileen Rowthorn, Eric W. Rowthorn, Rita B. Powers, Leonard Bernstein, Ludwig von Beethoven, Marney Goldsmith, Gladys Clayton, Richard Pettit, Mary Ann Pettit, Thomas Daye, Gretchen Pritchard, Murray Sidlin, William Shakespeare, Chris Clark, Salvador Dali, Ricardo Pimentel, Maude Holmes, Laura Ingalls Wilder, Charles Dickens, Sally F. Maryboy, William Stringfellow, C.S. Lewis, Irene Jackson-Brown, Isabel Murray, Kevin Leary, Cynthia DeLouise, Dorothy Yanick, Ruth Moore, Anthony Russo, Stephen S. Wilburn, John Dailinger, Doris Heelas, Edith Witcomb,

Kathleen Lowe, Georgia Carlson, Erna Cocchiaro, Ruth Redington, Tamara L. Guevara, Susan Ransom, Fritz Eichenberg, Chenda Korm, Jackie O'Neill, Ellen Stanley, Laura Mol, Frank Pinto, James Grasso, Nicholas Grasso, Carolyn Lewis, Willa Cather, Alexander Solzhenitsyn, Edna Swan, Evelyn Babb, Elie Wiesel, Carrie Cloutman, Hope Kirkpatrick, Philip Johnson, Edith Townsend, Beverly Fawcett, Paul Schattauer, Kevin Bee, Frances Carr, Kathleen Oberholzer, Bob Geldof, Will Mebane, Richard Fitzpatrick, Weston Robinson, Nelson Mandala, Margaret Mead, Martha S. Bentley, Edward Kennedy, Peggy Voris, Bettye Jo Harris, Joe, Lech Walesa, Robert Jefferies, Carolyn Jefferies, Betty Caceres, Mercedes Pujols, Joe Coelho, Jack Spaeth, Dorothy Dodge York, Gene Kadela, David Olivera, Paul Hodel, Kay Claiborn, Jean Allen Henderson, Karreem Mebane, Soren Kierkegaard, Chuck Shepard, Linn Bayne, Robert Meyer, Judith Gillespie, Peter Jennings, Nile Heermans, Roberta Walmsley, June Aziz, Corazon Aquino, Mark Patton, Kathy Hooker, V.S. Naipaul, A.B. Guthrie, Jr., Stephen King, Everdale Wright, Cynthia Roomy, Martin Buber, and Brigid M. Plunkett.

CONTENTS

THE LIBERATION OF THE LAITY

INTRODUCTION

This is a book about the laity, and it is written by a layperson. It is offered to the whole Church. I hope it will be widely read by those in the pew as well as by the leaders of the Church. Though I trust its contents will be deemed correct from a scholarly viewpoint, this work is to be considered as an educated—but not scholarly—assessment of the history, tradition, and current practices of the Church as seen through the prism of this particular layperson. Although I aspire to be a lay theologian, I do not in any way claim to be a biblical scholar, a liturgist, or a Church historian. Rather, I write as one who has read the scholarship and benefited from the hard work of others. On the basis of my reading and thinking, and my deep affection for the Church to which I owe much, I am now moved to share my thoughts. I do so in the hope that these reflections will resonate with the readers' and that the issues I raise will contribute to the remaking of a Church that will become, more and more, the loving community of the faithful, called and sent to be God's eyes and hands and hearts and minds in the world, for which Christ lived and died.

I shall be so bold as to suggest that it is the laity of the Church—coming to their full stature as Christians and as human beings—who can and should be the primary means through which the Church transforms itself to live God's life and accomplish God's will in society.

As long as the laity believe they *go* to church whereas the clergy *are* the Church, and as long as Church structures and practices allow the clergy to dominate Christ's ministry (in which all Christians ought to participate), the laity will fail to be what the Church might become and will continue to feed off the crumbs that fall from clerical tables. (Or they will take their own places at the clerical tables.)

A strong indication of the grievous state of institutional Churches is that most of them do not know how to handle their lay members who are serious about the faith, articulate, and thoughtful. It has been said innumerable times to this layperson that the Church, in time, either ordains its strong and vocal laypersons or it silences them.

Officials of Protestant churches throughout the U.S. are being inundated by genuinely religious people who sincerely feel their calls to ministry can come to full expression only through ordination. The call to ministry is often equated with the call to the ordained ministry. Because the pull toward ordination is so strong, remaining lay becomes, therefore, a conscious, often little-understood, and difficult choice. I and many other laypersons have been called on many times to explain why we remain lay. Ordination would be easier. It would be understood.

The laity of the Church are a voiceless, sightless, powerless, invisible mass, badgered—however subtly—by the clergy into passivity and compliance and then criticized by those same clergy for being so. We are believers whose historical roots have been kept from us. We have almost no lay models for Christian living that the Church recognizes and affirms. Many denominations have their calendars of saints—those exemplars of Christian living and dying whose stories, systematically recollected throughout the seasons of the Church year, help us along the way. But how many of us have noticed that these prayer cycles are almost exclusively devoted to ascetics, clergy, and monastics? The reflective layperson wonders why.

The laity are essentially persons without a history in which to be rooted. Without a shared experience, a common memory, a history, groups of persons cannot become a people. They remain just that—groups and little else; they are not a people. Certainly our history as laypersons—however fragmentary—*is* there, but unless we have access to it, for practical purposes it does not exist.

I hope the laity of the Church will recover their history and develop a genuine theology. This layperson has had to use the best talents of professional theologians to authenticate her statements and, in some places, to speak for her. In fact, scarcely a word of this book would have been written had it not been for the scholarly work of such theologians, Church historians, and liturgists as Hans Küng, Edward Schillebeeckx, John Macquarrie, Theodore Eastman; Michael Green, Durstan McDonald, Cyril C. Richardson, Louis Weil, Oscar Cullman, Henry Chadwick, Jürgen

Moltmann, Owen Chadwick, Roland H. Bainton, John Robinson, Jeffery Rowthorn, Clive Barrett, Juan Luis Segundo, Roland Allen, and Tissa Balasuriya. I am particularly indebted to such Latin American liberation theologians as Gustavo Gutiérrez and Leonardo Boff. Their profound influence on me will be readily apparent throughout the book. I am deeply grateful for their work and that of the many others also cited in the notes. Had this book not been dedicated solely to lay saints, these scholars certainly would have been added to the list. The name of one of them, Jeffery Rowthorn, would have been outlined in hearts and circled with garlands of roses, for he has been my true friend and colleague. After all, what other husband would have entered into a discussion of transubstantiation or "absolute ordination" over the breakfast table?

A word about inclusive (i.e. nonsexist) language: Many of the authorities quoted herein wrote their works before they became aware of the importance of inclusive language. Masculine though their pronouns are, I have nonetheless chosen to use their contributions because I felt the value of their insights far outweighed the linguistic considerations. I have, however, attempted to make *my* text as inclusive as possible.

In this book I refer to "the Church" in three ways: as a means of describing, in a broad way, Christ's Church; in referring to the denomination of which I am a member (the Episcopal Church); and in referring to the Roman Catholic and Lutheran Churches. Whenever another denomination is specified, I have so indicated.

Finally, like any other lay member of the Church, I have learned my lessons well. I know my place. I carry deep within me the quiet terror that in examining the Church closely—and particularly in criticizing it (however justly and constructively)—I am somehow "stepping out of line," moving into forbidden territory, forgetting on which side of the rood screen I belong, treading where I ought not to go. So in writing this book I have had to overcome very strong inner resistance. Even now, as the book's completion draws near, I have a strong impulse just to throw it away and pretend it never existed. Fearful though I am, I have done what I honestly felt I was being led to do: I have written what I believe had to be said. In doing so, I have taken heart from Edward Schillebeeckx's words, uttered when he published a book he believed would be controversial (it was!):

> By virtue of his task as a theologian, in critical service to the Church, he has that sometimes painful duty of showing the Church authorities whether their approach in fact takes account of all the features of what is actually a very complex set of problems. Here even the theologian in turn stands under the pastoral oversight of the leaders

of the Church; but this must not make him cowardly and prevent him from having his say. He must speak out even when he is convinced that in all probability the Church authorities will make other decisions. Each person has his or her own unalienable responsibility for acting honorably and in accord with conscience, aware of possible consequences which may follow, even for himself, in the Church.[1]

CHAPTER 1

THE MINISTERS OF THE CHURCH

Ministry is God acting through the people of God for
the life of the world.

—*God's People in Ministry,*
Lutheran Church in America

The laity are the prime ministers of the Church. They constitute up to 99 percent of church membership. They are the most typical, the most usual, the most regular, the most ordinary Christians. They are normative Christians. Clergy, in contrast, are neither average nor ordinary Christians. They are not usual. They are not, in general, the means through which the Church is presented to the world.

Through its laity the Church is present in every area of human activity. It is in offices, in schools and universities, in hospitals, in stores, in factories and hotels. The Church is present where political decisions are made: in courts, in state legislatures, in Congress. Through the laity the Church is present in conference rooms and executive suites; it is there when corporate questions are deliberated. On docks, in the streets, in bars and restaurants, on farms, in cities and towns and suburbs, the Church is present in every human undertaking.

Without its laity the Church has no place in the world. But whether or not Christ is represented in human activity is dependent on whether or not the laity genuinely represent him.

Christ is represented in an employee's concern for an employer, in a nurse listening to an anxious patient, when a teacher understandingly listens to a child's question, when the telephone is answered with warmth; in the meeting of minds, in laughter, when a trusted companion relieves one's worries. He is represented when anger is not repaid with anger, when the irritating individual is treated with kindness, when the stranger is welcomed, when the foreigner is treated as a neighbor. He is represented over the counter at the supermarket and over the gas pump. He is represented when the ambulance team responds swiftly and efficiently to the heart attack victim and when the realtor makes an honest sale. Christ is represented when the stranger helps the stranded motorist. He is represented when the widow comforts the bereaved, when the hungry one is served at table, when the little girl runs an errand for the old man. He is served when the gardener gives his produce to the soup kitchen, when the paperboy lingers a minute to chat with the lonely lady on his route.

Christ is present when his people listen to the lonely, the helpless, the ill; when his people listen to children's dreams, to the elderly in their despair. He is present in the tortured faces of the broken-hearted, in huddled, homeless, hungry humanity. He is represented in the response of his people—in what they say and how they say it, in what they hear and how they hear it, in what they think and how they think it, in their being and their doing.

> Every time a human being opens to God and the other, wherever true love exists and egoism is surpressed, when human beings seek justice, reconciliation, and forgiveness, there we have true Christianity. . . . The true Christian is one who lives that which Christ lived, that for which he was imprisoned, condemned, and executed. . . . It is not those who are Christian who are good, true and just. Rather the good, the true, and the just are Christian. . . . Christianity is concretized in the world whenever people open themselves like Christ to the totality of reality.[1]

Or Christ may not be present. It all depends on Christians—the greatest number of whom are lay Christians—and whether or not they are *open* to Christ in the other and whether or not they truly *represent* Christ.

> In the last analysis, the Church speaks to and acts upon the world through her laity. Without a dynamic laity conscious of its personal ministry to the world, the Church, in effect, does not speak or act. No amount of social action by priests and religious can ever be an adequate substitute for enhancing lay responsibility.[2]

The Catechism of the Episcopal Church, for example, states that "the ministers of the Church are lay persons, bishops, priests and deacons."[3] In that order. Laypersons are the Church's front line. They are called to bear witness to the sovereignty of Christ in everyday life. Their ministries come first. It is no accident that laypersons are listed first, before bishops, priests, and deacons, because they are first in making contact with the world for which Christ lived and died.

The Church, of course, needs all its ministries, each of which has its particular function in the community of faith. When properly balanced, the entire congregation carries out the work of the Church and is engaged in service: presbyters (priests) particularly as pastors of congregations, laypersons especially in the everyday workings of the world. The *entire Church* is the ministering community, *not* the ordained minister representing the Church, *not* the clergy acting on its behalf.

The community of faith, rightly understood, is not an association of people gathered around a presbyter, for, as the New Testament states, the *whole* people of God has become a priesthood: "You are a chosen race, a royal priesthood . . . a people claimed by God for his own" (1 Pet. 2:9).

The very early Church knew no hierarchy of ministries, nor orders, nor ranks. As Hans Küng points out, in the New Testament the word "priest" is not used to describe someone who holds office in the Church.[4] Neither does the term "layperson" appear. In fact, its first recorded use was in A.D. 95, when Clement of Rome described the ordinary membership of the Church. Until then there had been no need to distinguish between members of the body. The neologism was an acknowledgement of the emergence of an organized group of clergy, distinct from other Christians.

The development of the clerical class, as early as the early fourth century, also resulted in the devaluation of the New Testament understanding of the "Priesthood of All Believers," the idea of the Church as the Body of Christ and the ministering community of the faithful without rank.

The ministry of presbyters cleaved from the ministry of the entire congregation. Divided, clerical and lay ministries developed along separate— and unequal—lines. Once set apart from the general membership of the Body, clerical ministries became increasingly professional. Specialized education and formal qualifications for ministry assumed greater importance. A separate and elitist form of spirituality based on ascetics, monastics, and mystics developed, to which few laypeople could relate. And little by little, the professional ministers arrogated to themselves functions that, in the early Church, had been the province of all. The growth and development of the laity, in contrast, was stunted. Laypersons lost touch with their heritage of full-bodied ministerial responsibility as part of the universal "Priesthood of All Believers," and the laity of the Church are now but a pale shadow of what they once were.

One would have thought inequality in the Church to be a God-ordained condition, for Pope Gregory XVI (1831-46) stated,

> No one can deny that the Church is an unequal society in which
> God destined some to be govenors and others to be servants. The
> latter are the laity; the former clergy.[5]

Such was the mindset of the Church that in 1906 Pope Pius X stated in
an encyclical,

> The Church essentially is an unequal society. That is, it is a society
> formed by two categories of persons: pastors and flock. . . . As far
> as the multitude is concerned, they have no other duty than to let
> themselves be led.[6]

Unempowered and passive, laypersons stepped back and allowed the
professional ministers to control the mind, the voice, the heart of the
Church, while they sat helplessly on the fringe. And they have believed
the myths propagated by seventeen hundred years of clericalization: that
laity *go* to church, but clergy *are* the Church; that professional ministers
are more religious, more holy, and are the exclusive mediators between
God and the people; that clergy alone celebrate the Eucharist, whereas
laity only receive communion; that presbyters (i.e., priests, professionally
ordained ministers) presiding at Eucharist represent God; that clergy have
special access to God; that ascetics, monastics, and mystics are *the* models
of Christian spirituality.

The shame is that the laity have believed these myths; the scandal is
that the clergy have not corrected them. The scandal is that the clergy
have failed to teach the laity that they are, in every way, just as much
the Church as any ordained minister. The scandal is that clergy have
considered themselves more holy and religious than the laity and have
failed to communicate that holiness belongs to no special order or rank
in the Church and may, in fact, be most manifest in the least of the world's
children: the poor, the weak, the meek, the lowly, the downhearted, and
the outcast. The scandal is that the clergy have failed to teach the people
that the ordained person represents Christ no more or less than any other
Christian. The scandal is that clergy have not adequately taught the people
that the ordinary Christian's intercession to God on behalf of others is
every bit as efficacious as the professional minister's. The scandal is that
the clergy have failed to teach the people that the entire community of
the faithful celebrates the Lord's supper; presbyters merely preside at the
celebration. The scandal is that the clergy have failed to teach the people
that in presiding at Eucharist they speak in the name of the *Church;* they
do not replace God in the sacramental act. The scandal is that the clergy
have not understood the laity's need for a spirituality of and in the world
that affirms their response to God in everyday life. The scandal is that

the clerical domination of the Church has so choked the vitality out of ordinary Christians that churches have become repositories for the passive and the compliant.

> One of the difficulties laity find with most churches is that really open controversy is nearly always considered wicked and disloyal. And laypersons are polite people and so they don't normally want to stand up against clergy or other church members, and so they quietly vote with their feet. I have many, many times wished that I could just leave alone difficult church arguments, and I know very many of my friends who don't want to be "awkward." Somebody once whispered to me in a church in Canada, "Mark, just slip your mind into neutral." But this is not true fellowship. This is something less; and if we are not careful we get a church organization dominated by some leaders and by the "loyal" laity; and the rest just keep quiet or leave.[7]

And finally, the scandal is that the clergy have blamed their victims. They have condemned—however subtly—the laity for waiting on them to be authorized for ministry. But how could it have been otherwise? The laity have learned their lessons only too well.

Vatican II, social-liberation movements of the 1960s and 1970s, and the recovery of some of the theology of the early Church as expressed in the liturgical reforms of the last two decades have helped somewhat to restore the laity in the Christian community. The respective roles of laypersons and presbyters, however, are still distorted. The concerns of professional ministers continue to occupy the Church's energies. The clergy's power—grossly disproportionate to their numbers—has continued to foster a passive and submissive laity. It has turned laypersons into recipients of professional ministry, whereas it ought to have recognized and supported laity as ministers in their own right. Presbyters wanting to serve and people wanting to be served have led to an incestuous domestic relationship.

> The hegemony of the presbyterate is so strong that it absorbs all the power and focus of ministry into itself, turning the laity into willing clients for ministry rather than ministers of Christ, a priestly people. . . . The laity are established as second class citizens, a clergy support group, patients for the ministrations of clergy, and a baptized proletariat beneath the ecclesiastical aristocracy.[8]

Some might argue that lay ministry has been recovered in recent years. Unfortunately, laypersons and clergy alike have, in large measure, interpreted it as urging a more active lay role in the institution of the Church and in liturgical celebrations. And though greater lay participation in liturgy is indeed an important development, the reform of ministry has hardly begun. The laypersons' contributions in the parish must always be considered secondary to the far more difficult work of practicing ministry in the everyday life of the world. Moreover, the laity have sat idle and allowed the clergy to define their ministries for them. Much of what is done in the name of lay ministry has, in reality, led to the development of a "clericalized laity"—a laity turned inward—absorbed in the institution of the Church while neglecting the outward service of Christ in society.

The devaluation of lay ministry has also had a negative effect on clergy. Clergy have become isolated, withdrawn into themselves as a group, disoriented in the community of faith. Their development as a class apart from the whole ministerial body has resulted in their becoming over-extended, subject to unreasonable expectations of the laity, and expected to see to all the spiritual needs of the congregation while sometimes neglecting their own. No major denomination is without its share of clergy who at midlife and midcareer have become bitter, broken, disillusioned, angry. It is the legacy of the age-old split between clergy and laypersons and the separation of professional ministers from the whole ministerial body that is the Church.

> The clergy/laity distinction has set up many false problems for the Church, and will go on doing so as long as it is retained, since it represents a principle alien to the nature of the Church . .[9]

The hard task of describing the essential role of laypersons in the institutional Church and, more important yet, of those living out their ministries in the world ought to benefit clergy by relieving them of unnecessary burdens and the need to rationalize the scope of their ministry. In addition, a redefinition of clerical ministries would create space for the laity to function according to their gifts for service.

> The health, vitality and wholeness not only of the Church, but of the world, is dependent upon the Church's recovery of the biblical conviction of the priesthood of all believers—the full ministry of the whole people of God.[10]

What is needed is nothing less than a bold reform of ministry—both lay and ordained—and nothing more than the will and the courage to accomplish it.

CHAPTER 2

THE PRIESTHOOD OF THE CHURCH

You are a chosen race, a royal priesthood . . . a people
claimed by God.

—1 Peter 2:9

MINISTRY

The fundamental reality of ministry is the ministry of the *entire*
servant Church. . . . Basic to any real understanding of specific,
full or part time, professional or amateur ministries within the faith
community is the feeling that the *whole* church is ministerial, is
ministry.[1]

Ministry ought to be like a barn-raising. The community of farmers
from around the countryside gathers at the farm where the new barn is
to be built. They build the frame, carefully measuring each piece of wood,
sawing, and nailing it all together while the frame still rests on the ground.
Then ropes are attached, and all farmers, pulling together, raise the barn.
However strong or expert in the fine art of barn building a particular
farmer might be, it would be impossible for him, by himself, to raise the
barn. It couldn't be done. But a group of farmers, pulling together, are
strong enough to raise the sturdy structure. In any group of farmers there
will be a variety of talents. Some will have steady eyes for measuring;
others will be proficient in carpentry. Children can drive nails. One farmer
might shingle a roof better than another; another might be able to make
strong doors and a secure loft. There will be others who bring in the
lemonade during the day and provide a bountiful banquet at the end of
it to celebrate the raising of one more barn.

Ministry at its best is like this: *All* the farmers with *all* their gifts
together build the barn—the Body of Christ.

The good news of the New Testament is that there are no longer a
priestly clerical class and an unpriestly laity. All priesthood—lay and

ordained—is derived from the one, holy, and eternal priesthood of Christ, and all ministry is Christ's ministry in which the faithful are privileged to participate according to their gifts.

> In that one supreme moment in his life when Jesus did offer sacrifice once and for all, he gathered into himself the whole meaning of priesthood and sacrifice, and obliterated forever the need of a priestly caste. The result of that action, and his entirely original contribution was, for the first time in the history of religion, to enable an entire people to be priest. Is this not one of the biggest differences between Christianity and all other religions on the face of the earth.?[2]

This priesthood of Christ—and the priesthood of the whole Church— contrasts sharply with the Old Testament understanding of priesthood originating in a priestly class. Christ's priesthood is not inherited, for Christ was descended from Judah, a tribe to which Moses made no reference in speaking about priests. Rather, Christ was a priest from Melchizedek, of which little or nothing is known. "He has no father, no mother, no lineage; his years have no beginnings; his life no end" (Heb. 7:3). Just as Christ had no special lineage, so with us. Through Christ a priestly class has been abolished forever; through him all believers share in a universal priesthood. And because all believers share in essential and radical equality in the one eternal priesthood of all believers, the Church is, therefore, that community of the priesthood of Christ which, filled with his spirit, became his body in the world.

> Every Christian is a priest for the world. . . . The priesthood of all believers is a fellowship in which each Christian, instead of living for himself, lives before God for others and is in turn supported by others.[3]

Any discussion of the body of Christ in which *all* members have their roles and functions and gifts must begin with St. Paul's description of the Christian community in 1 Corinthians: "For by one spirit we were all baptized into one body . . . and all were made to drink of the one Spirit" (1 Cor. 12:13). There he described the body as consisting of many parts. Some may seem more important, others less than others, but the *whole* body is dependent on the functioning of *every* part. Though St. Paul distinguishes between leadership functions within the body and gifts for ministry, *all* are intended to benefit the community of faith. "To each is given the manifestation of the Spirit for the common good" (1 Cor. 12:7).

The first Christians were urban Jews solidly rooted in the continuing tradition of Israel. Their task was to convince their fellow Jews that, with Christ, the Messiah had come and that Old Testament prophecy had been fulfilled. In the Roman world there were many cults; Christianity, in earliest times, appeared merely as one of them.

The earliest churches were the members' homes; the first Bibles simply Old Testaments. Authority resided in Scripture and in oral tradition. Jesus' words were circulated by oral tradition even after being written down in the Gospels.

It was considered of utmost importance that the entire Christian community gather in one place on the first day of the week—the day of Christ's resurrection—which was also when he reappeared to his disciples who had gathered for a meal. The Lord's Day became, therefore, a celebration of Christ's resurrection, an Easter to be celebrated once a week.[4]

The earliest celebrations of the Eucharist probably took place in the context of meals. The service consisted of readings from the Old Testament and recollections of Jesus' life and ministry. The president (bishop) preached, and the kiss of peace was passed among those gathered. Bread and wine mixed with water were brought to the president, who led the people in the Great Thanksgiving and in what we would now call the "Eucharistic Prayer." This prayer's form soon became fixed. Hippolytus' prayer (c. 215), on which the contemporary prayer is based, bears repeating:

> Remembering therefore his death and resurrection, we offer you this bread and cup, giving you thanks that *you have counted us worthy to stand before you and minister to you as priests.*[5]

The elements having been blessed by the president, the celebration continued with the communion, distributed by the deacons. No member of the community was to be left out of the celebration of the Eucharist, and the first Christians took great pains to ensure that every member received it. Leftovers were taken to those who were unable to be at the gathering, the sick and the imprisoned. If there was sufficient bread, the Christians carried it to their homes, where it was consumed after daily prayers during the week.

The pattern of leadership in the early Church—as now—was derived from Christ's commission to the apostles. Wayne Meeks has pointed out that Acts of the Apostles and Paul's Letters make no mention of formal offices in early Christian congregations.[6] Neither was there a formal process of selecting leaders. Those who had capacities for leadership exercised it; for those who did not, there were plenty of other necessary functions to perform. There was no hierarchy; rather, Paul lists the variety of gifts for ministry: wisdom, knowledge, faith, gifts of healing, the working of miracles, prophecy, the ability to distinguish between spirits, various tongues (1 Cor. 12). Paul talks about leadership—about apostles, prophets, teachers, helpers, administrators (1 Cor. 12). In Ephesians 4 he adds evangelists and pastors to the list. He talks about the functions necessary to the community of faith: exhortation, the making of contributions (donations), giving aid, acts of mercy and cheerfulness (Rom. 12). All these capacities were generously given by God that they be used to build the community of faith "for the common good" (1 Cor. 12:7).

In imagining the life of the early Church through the world of St. Paul, one is forcibly struck by the sense of equality in which the gifts, abilities, and contributions of all members are valued and appreciated. But attractive as this scheme may have been, it could not continue. According to Meeks:

> No group can persist for any appreciable time without developing some patterns of leadership, some differentiation of roles among its members, some means of managing conflict, some ways of articulating shared values and norms, and some sanctions to assure acceptable levels of conformity to those norms. . . . We would like to know what sorts of persons were able to issue commands or make recommendations that would ordinarily be accepted by members of the church Paul and his associates founded. And we want to know why the followers obeyed.[7]

By the second century, as structure emerged, "apostles" and "prophets" evolved roughly into "bishops" and "deacons" (bishops being the leaders of the congregations and deacons the servants of the Christian communities). Originally bishops presided over single congregations, but the latter proliferated so quickly that often a bishop had to oversee several. This arrangement soon became impractical, and the bishops began to appoint presbyters (priests) to assume responsibility for some of their domain. Thus emerged an additional tier in the Church hierarchy. Its organizational structure came to consist of bishops, presbyters, and deacons.

Presbyters were those who, first and foremost, presided over the life of the community. In accordance with that role, they also presided over the Eucharist. It is important that this sequence be fully understood. The person who gave the community its unity, who was its symbol of unity, therefore also presided over the sacrament of Church unity—the Eucharist. In that order.

by an Episcopal Church-commissioned consultation on the ordained ministry (1982), which stated:

> If anything emerged with startling clarity during this interdisciplinary gathering of scholars, parish clergy and bishops, it was that the terms "priesthood" and "ordained ministry" are not synonymous (contrary to popular use). . . . The key distinction is between the priesthood of the People of God, the Christian community, and the ordered ministry commonly called the priesthood. It is awkward to use the term "presbyter," but it serves the dual purpose of indicating that Christians are priestly persons by virtue of their baptism and that questions about the ordained ministry or "the priest" are questions about pastoral leadership in the community of Jesus Christ.[14]

An intriguing question arises: If the whole people of God, filled with the spirit of Christ and sharing in his high priesthood, has become a priesthood, are all Christians priests? The answer is yes and no. Yes, the priesthood of all is borne out in the wording of Hippolytus' Eucharistic Prayer, the earliest known Christian liturgy, which contains the phrase "you have counted us worthy to stand before you and minister to you as priests." Also, *The Apostolic Constitutions,* Book 8, of a slightly later date (c. 375) states:

> Remembering then his passion and death and resurrection . . . we offer you, King and God, according to his commandment, this bread and this cup, giving you thanks through him that you have deemed us worthy to stand before you and *to be your priests.*[15]

We speak of our membership in Christ's priesthood during every baptism service, when we welcome the newly baptized with this prayer:

> We receive you into the household of God. Confess the faith of Christ crucified, proclaim his resurrection, and *share with us in his eternal priesthood.*[16]

No, individual Christians are not called priests because, according to the New Testament, Christ and the Christian community alone are priestly. The members are at the service of Christ and the priestly people of God, but we as individuals are never said to be priests.[17] So priesthood belongs to the Church—to *all* members of the Church, lay and ordained alike— but it is enough that we simply call ourselves Christians.

Acts of the Apostles and Paul's letters mention many people who were essential to the life of the expanding Church. They were: Priscilla and Aquila (Acts 18:26), Tryphaena and Tryphosa (Rom. 16:3), husbands and wives; Stephanas' family, the first converts in Achia—"They have devoted themselves to the service of the saints" (1 Cor. 16:5)—and Philip's four daughters, who were prophets (Acts 21:9); Phoebe, Epaenetus and Mary, Andronicus, Junias, Ampliatus, Urbanus, Stachys, Apelles, and the families of Aristobulus and Narcissus; Herodion, Persis, and Rufus and his mother; Asyncritus, Phlegon, Hermes, Patrobas, Hermas, Philologus, Julia, Nereus and his sister, and Olympas; Timothy, Lucius, Jason and Sosipater, Gaius, Erastus and Quartus (Rom. 16).

Paul called some of them "apostles"—his general title to describe not only the original twelve but many others who led congregations. There was no particular order, rank, or distinction. All that mattered was that they were members of the body.

EARLIEST CHRISTIAN COMMUNITIES

Early Christians were easily identifiable by the quality of their lives. It was Tertullian, one of the early church fathers, who once quoted a pagan as saying, "See how these Christians love one another." As already noted, every week Christians took the communion to the sick and the imprisoned. They were well known both for their charity and their hospitality. Whatever they had they readily shared with the poor, the widows, and the orphans. In fact, the primary function of church treasuries was to provide for the needs of the poor. Christians were hospitable to travelers; to be welcomed into Christian homes, strangers on the road had only to give proof of their faith.

Evangelism was the responsibility of every Christian. "We have seen apostles and wandering prophets, nobles and paupers, intellectuals and fishermen all taking part in the primary task committed by Christ to his Church. The ordinary people of the Church saw it as their job: Christianity was supremely a lay movement, spread by informal missionaries."[18]

Certainly as important in commending the faith was the distinctively godly lifestyle of ordinary Christians living out their faith in their day-to-day lives. Undoubtedly, their example was a powerful witness to the fullness of Christ and his care for humanity. Christian communities were indeed Christ's body in the world.

The community of the priesthood of all believers only makes sense if in fact its members live out the consequences of their faith in concrete ways. In Jürgen Moltmann's words:

> If all Christians were active members, this church *for* the people would cease to exist, and a new church *of* the people would come into being.[19]

The quest for God, therefore, begins and ends in persons. There can be no authentic search for godliness in itself; only the search for humanness, because it is in the flesh that we seek and are sought by God.

But what of those who have been prevented from giving their gifts to others? When people are not taken seriously, when their contributions and talents are rejected, when their voices are not heard, when their insights go unnoticed, when they have been prevented from giving their gifts, their humanity is denied. If their humanity is denied, God also is denied.

The Church in North America is in desperate need of a liberation movement, a movement through which the laity can regain their sight, their voice, their free movement in the body of Christ. The Church must be liberated from the clerical captivity of the clergy. It must be liberated from the oppression by the clerical minority who prevent the full and free participation of the lay majority. This movement has already begun in small ways, and it shares the same basic characteristics of all such movements. It has as its goal the restoration of the New Testament understanding of a priesthood of all believers and the revitalization of the fundamental reality of ministry as "the ministry of the *entire* servant church."[2]

> The liberation of man and the growth of the Kingdom both are directed toward complete communion of men with God and of men among themselves. . . . The growth of the Kingdom is a process which occurs historically *in* liberation, insofar as liberation means a greater fulfillment of man.[3]

In speaking of the liberation of the laity, I am aware of many problems, the major one being that many laypersons are not even aware of the need for change; seventeen centuries of clerical oppression have left them blind, mute, and paralyzed. Perhaps they sense that the Christian community is not all it might be, but they have difficulty in identifying just what is wrong. And how could one expect it to be otherwise? How can laypersons know what they might be without first knowing what they once were? How can they find a voice they never knew they had? How can they reclaim a ministry they are only dimly aware of having lost? And how can they take up their places in a priesthood to which they never knew they belonged in the first place? In short, how is the humanity of all persons to be restored, and how is the Church to be rebuilt?

The process of liberation is the same whether one speaks of a race, a group of persons, or a sex. It is a movement toward the full expression of personhood that allows all parties to become more human. The insights of the Brazilian educator Paulo Freire are useful in considering the need for a liberation of the Church for the ministry of all its members:

> To surmount the situation of oppression, men must first critically recognize its causes, so that through transforming action they can create a new situation, one which makes possible a fuller humanity. But the struggle to be more fully human has already begun in the authentic struggle to transform the situation. Although the situation of oppression is a dehumanized and dehumanizing totality affecting both the oppressors and those whom they oppress, it is the latter who must, from their stifled humanity, wage for both the struggle for a fuller humanity; the oppressor, who is himself dehumanized because he dehumanizes others, is unable to lead this struggle.[4]

Some might say it is overstating the case to claim that clergy are the oppressors and laity the oppressed. So let us make several things clear: It is primarily the *system* that oppresses. It took hundreds of years for the Church to become clericalized, and the present generation of clergy cannot be blamed for the ills of the institution they inherited. To continue to oppress the laity, however, after having become aware of the oppression *would* make them blameworthy. Also, to say that clergy have stifled the laity does not mean the former are in any way bad pepole. Indeed, many clergy feel there is much wrong with the institutional Church, but they are at a loss to know what to do about it. They do not realize that in depersonalizing the laity they also have become depersonalized. The clericalization of the Church is a problem for all Christians.

Certainly the clergy, in most cases, are not even aware of the ways they oppress the laity. It is therefore the latter's responsibility—however difficult it may be for them—to demonstrate to the clergy how the Church has been clericalized and to be the prime movers in remedying the condition. Let us not forget that before Martin Luther King white people thought there was nothing wrong in demanding that black people ride in the backs of public buses. Indeed, the majority of Americans then were unaware of how the white majority oppressed black people. It took members of that minority to sensitize their fellow Americans to the inhumanity inflicted on them by indifferent or prejudiced whites. Also, the public had a romantic notion of the Native American as the "noble savage," until Vine Deloria (the son of an Episcopal priest) called attention to the degradation and deprivation visited on the Indians by the dominant population. And it took feminist Betty Friedan to elucidate the meaning of male oppression of women. The laity need their Martin Luther Kings, their Vine Delorias, their Betty Friedans, who have the courage to risk

the struggles, the misunderstandings, and the torments that are the con-
comitants of any true change.

The laity are weak, they are paralyzed, they are blind, they are voiceless. Nonetheless, out of their weakness they must find the strength to
liberate the Church from its inhumanity, from the bondage of clericalism,
so it can become, once again, the loving community of human beings
that Christ loved so much. The laity, however weak, must seize the
initiative for change, because the clergyperson "who is himself dehuman-
ized because he dehumanizes others, is unable to lead the struggle."[5]

> Only those who truly believe that they have something to offer
> can experience themselves as spiritually adult. As long as someone
> feels that he or she is only an object of someone else's generosity,
> no dialogue, no mutuality, no authentic community can exist.[6]

Only when laypersons come to the realization that they are now but
a pale shadow of the full-bodied Christians they were meant to be, only
when they learn what they have lost, only when they recover their voice
and their free movement in Christ's body, only then will they grow to
their full stature as human beings who live for the world for which Christ
lived and died. Only then will the Church be truly the Church.

Every liberation movement—whether that of American blacks, of
Native Americans, of women, or of the Latin American poor—has at some
stage in its development necessarily returned to its origins. A group cannot
become a people unless it has a history, unless it has gone on a journey
to discover its roots. Such journeys into the past are attempts to uncover
beginnings, to discover stories of a people, the tradition of a people, the
causes for change in the historical conditions and perceptions of a people.
The Old Testament is a treasury of stories of a people on a journey toward
liberation. Our goal as lay Christians is the reclamation of our place in
that historical journey. It is to find once again our place in that history,
that tradition, so we can continue in Christ and with each other on God's
journey through time and eternity.

> The scope and gravity of the process of liberation is such that
> to ponder its significance is really to examine the meaning of
> Christianity itself and the mission of the Church in the world.[7]

Christianity is essentially a lay movement founded by a lay Jew who
was neither a Sadducee (a member of the priestly class, a political aristo-
crat), nor a Pharisee (a keeper of the law), nor a scribe (an interpreter
of the law, a sort of canon lawyer). Jesus Christ was not of the priestly,
political, moral, or legal elite. The unfolding history of Christianity is a

tale of resistance to both Jewish tendencies (captivity of the faith by the priestly class and the maintenance of a legal interpretation of the Gospel) and Greek tendencies (esoteric knowledge, mystery religions and ceremonies). As Robert Escarpit has said, "However strange it may seem, the Christian revolution is lay and anticlerical."[8]

Furthermore, most if not all of the struggles (including the current one) in the development of Christianity have been to protect the faith from Judaizing or Hellenizing. They have been protests against those forces that would take the Gospel (and its faithful living) out of ordinary persons' grasp and so deny its quintessential lay character.

Just as Jesus was about the recovery and the fulfillment of universal lay Jewish vocation, so with us today. We are about exactly what Jesus was about: the radical recovery of lay vocation in our time. Jesus had the highest expectations of ordinary people. He bypassed the experts and the professionals—the Sadducees, the Pharisees, the scribes—so that the goals of the Gospel might be attained. As with Jesus, so must it be with us.

The next chapter is a brief account of the historical development of the Church's clericalization, for only if clericalization is fully understood as the dehumanizing process it is—one that denies the very essence of the Gospel—will there be any hope for the transformation of the Church.

CHAPTER 4

THE CLERICAL CAPTIVITY
OF THE CHURCH

The idea of a Priesthood of All Believers gradually came
to be almost forgotten by the faithful and by most
theologians.

—Hans Küng, *The Church*

Christianity proved to be a remarkably successful movement. Before it
was three hundred years old it had spread throughout Syria, Asia Minor,
and Greece. There were probably Christians in Pompeii before A.D. 79.
By A.D. 250 there were about one hundred episcopal sees in Italy alone.[1]
By the early fourth century the faith had reached as far west as Britain.
All this was accomplished primarily by the apostolic zeal of the masses
of Christians who were so enthusiastic about the Gospel that they spread
it informally and easily. Some carried the faith with them as they traveled
the trade routes; others took it wherever they met people—in the marketplaces, at village wells, in every center of human activity. Christians lived
and conducted themselves as people who had received a prized gift, a
special possession, which, of course, they had. Their lives had been
transformed from within, and they lived and worshipped together in
loving fellowship. Their faith, their new way of being, was attractive to
others. It was contagious. Christians did not have to work to become
evangelists; they did so naturally, by word and deed and bearing. According to Harnack, "We cannot hesitate to believe that the great mission
of Christianity was in reality accomplished by the means of informal
missionaries."[2] And in Michael Green's words:

> The very disciples themselves were, significantly, laymen, devoid
> of formal theological or rhetorical training. Christianity was from
> its inception a lay movement, and so it continued for a remarkably
> long time. . . . In contrast to the present day when Christianity is
> highly intellectualized and dispensed by a professional clergy to

a constituency increasingly confined to the middle class. In the early days the faith was spread by informal evangelists and had its greatest appeal among the working classes.[3]

CONSTANTINE COURTS CHRISTIANITY

The Romans had always been highly tolerant of the many religions coexisting throughout the Roman Empire. Christians, like the adherents of the other religions and cults, were free to worship and to convert others as they chose. They had only to accept the divinity of the emperor. That was a big "only," however, and many faithful Christians came into sharp conflict with the state. They would neither offer sacrifices to the emperor nor pledge him ultimate allegiance. They would not denounce their faith, even if loyalty to the Gospel cost them their lives. They would not serve as soldiers, for they would not bear arms. Sons of soldiers, according to Roman law, were required to join the army. The story of a young soldier's son, a Christian called Maximilanus, is typical. When ordered to enroll and be equipped for service, Maximilanus told the proconsul:

> "I have a conscientious objection to military service: I am a Christian." The pro-consul insisted he be equipped anyway and the young man repeated his objections: "I cannot serve; I cannot sin against my conscience; I am a Christian. I will not do it; I cannot serve." And the pro-consul: "Serve or you will lose your life." Maximilanus: "I will not serve. You may behead me but I will not serve the powers of this world. I will serve my God."[4]

So, like so many other faithful and courageous Christians, this unwilling soldier was martyred.

Persecutions and martyrdoms unified the early Christians. The adherents sheltered and protected each other; they remained loyal to each other and, when necessary, paid the ultimate price of death.

After a severe rash of persecutions at the hands of Diocletian and other emperors, years of unrest in the Empire, the breakdown of civil order, the collapse of the economy, and repeated invasions by barbarians, the celebrated Constantine the Great succeeded to the throne (A.D. 285-337). He was successful in reuniting the Empire and in ushering in an era—brief but important—of relative calm and stability.

Constantine believed that the Christian God had given him victory, and out of gratitude he favored Christianity above his subjects' many other religions. Although he did not make Christianity the official religion of the empire, he wanted to give it a prominent standing among the others.

He identified with his new faith and put his entire influence behind it. Constantine moved the imperial capital from Rome in the West to Byzantium in the East, renamed it Constantinople, and rebuilt it as a Christian city. He had two magnificent cathedrals built, one dedicated to the apostles and the other to peace. He financed basilicas in Rome and Bethlehem, as well as new copies of the Bible.[5] Also, in making appointments to high offices in the state, Constantine gave preference to Christians.[6] This preferential treatment greatly increased Christianity's influence throughout the empire; the Church, in effect, became a department of the state.

This sudden and dramatic change in Christianity's political and social status proved to be a significant—though not altogether desirable—turning point. From Constantine onward, the character, the texture, the cohesiveness of the Christian movement changed markedly. Worshiping in a huge cathedral or a mighty basilica, for example, did not have the same feel as that in the intimacy of a home or small meeting hall. In A.D. 321 Sunday was declared a public holiday.[7] And since the faith had become acceptable, the people did not need to be as dependent on each other for their safety as they had been. Needing each other less, they lost their vital sense of solidarity.

The social status of the clergy changed markedly, too. In contrast to the early days when the people freely elected their bishops, the emperor began appointing bishops to the great cities and gave them some civil authority. The bishops who came from other churches to participate in consecrations became more important than the members of the local congregation. The ordinary people—the laity—began to be squeezed out of active and full participation in the community of faith.

As the power of the clergy grew, the power of the whole people of God waned.[8] Bishops became "distinguished." The Council of Arles in A.D. 314 addressed the Bishop of Rome by the title "most glorious," the phrase formerly used to refer only to the most distinguished persons, such as members of the imperial family. Each bishop came to have staff, mitre, and pallium. Kissing the bishop's hand began as a custom in the fourth century, though it was not until the fifth century that the practice of kissing his ring evolved.[9] In short, many new reasons had evolved for becoming a Christian, and even for seeking office in the Church, other than mere faith in Jesus Christ.[10]

The Church had won its freedom from a persecuting State, only to surrender this freedom to the Christian head of the State.[11]

ASCETICS AND MONASTICS

The First-Century Christians, a persecuted minority, looked for the coming of the kingdom. They believed it would come during their life-time, and they prepared themselves for a new and better age. But the world did not end! By the second century there were virgins and ascetics who lived as part of the Christian community, alongside the other, less pure folk. Virginity was coming to be thought of as necessary to a truly disciplined life.[12] In time, the pursuit of perfection came to be seen by these purists as a course of action that was being steadily undermined and hindered by the worldly distractions of ordinary church members.

Christians' lack of a distinctive identity apart from the secular society led to lax discipline in congregations, which were now composed of saints *and* sinners. This in turn resulted in the emergence of a double standard of Christian life. The historian Eusebius gave voice to the principle of the distinction between the higher, or superior, life of the Christian, who trained and disciplined himself or herself like an athlete, and the ordinary, or inferior, life of the masses of Christians. Ordinary Christians were considered more human, more earthy; they married, worked in secular occupations; they served in the army and held public office. Above the ways of these earthlings was the better course, a way to commune with God, a way that involved celibacy, aloofness from the affairs of the world, and wholehearted devotion to worship and the service of God.[13] The age of martyrdom had ended with Constantine's reign. The monk replaced the martyr, and ascetic and monastic life came to be equated with, and placed on the same level as, martyrdom.[14]

By the fourth century, Christianity had become a worldwide move-ment, and by the nature of things such a movement could not remain purely other-worldly. So virgins and ascetics, once found in the congre-gations, now broke away to pursue holiness in the loneliness of the desert. The term "martyr" came to be applied to anyone who lived a genuinely self-sacrificing life.[15] Disciplining the body, conquering sin, fighting demons (both internal and external), renouncing self, contemplating God—these were the ideals of asceticism. To live this sort of life, solitude was required, and human society was considered distracting.

> The journey through the desert corresponds to the gradual stripping away of the natural life and the discovery of the spiritual life. . . .
> Eventually the purified soul enters the more mystical region and reaches spiritual ecstasy.[16]

With the rise of the double standard in Christian life and practice and the solitary search for holiness there came a basic shift in the understanding of Christian community. "During the third and early fourth centuries, the idea of sanctity became less corporate and more individualistic."[17] From community to individual, from shared experience to solitary journey, from serving the social needs of the world to seeking lonely perfection, from holy to more holy—the basic understanding of Christian community had radically changed. It was a far cry from the early conception of the religious community as the priesthood of all believers, and it cast a long shadow over the subsequent development of the Church.

Asceticism led to monasticism. Ascetics, living apart in isolated cells and caves, began to join each other for worship. They banded together to raise food for their own use and to make products to be sold in the cities. The money they earned went to purchase the necessities they could not produce. As monasticism took hold and gained followers and as the urban areas expanded outward, the deserts became more and more densely populated. It was a movement that began in a small way in Egypt and spread to the West, and as it grew it became structured and organized. Though it could have been considered a lay movement because almost all the early monks were not ordained, the monastic lifestyle became a parallel expression of Christian life and community.

Certainly monasticism had its excesses, but those believers who took to the desert to follow the spiritual life were, after all, the more serious-minded and devout Christians. And so it is not for the solitary pursuit of the holy life as such that one criticizes the ascetic-monastic movement; rather, it is because of the effect the absence of these Christians had on the urban congregations they left behind. The congregations were left bereft of godly examples of Christian living and believing.

ONE THOUSAND YEARS' PRELUDE TO REFORM

The developments of the patristic period—from the apostolic age through the fifth century—set the pattern for the development of the Church that would continue right up to the Protestant Reformation. The consequences of absolute ordination, presbyters without people, the social acceptance of the Church, asceticism and monasticism, and the double standard of Christian living unfolded and worked themselves out throughout the Dark and Middle Ages.

> Although certain changes took place during the Middle Ages, none had the importance of those which occurred in the course of the fifth century: these were the decisive steps [discussed above] which the Church took as she evolved from the patristic to the medieval age.[18]

The focus of Church development shifted from the conception of the whole Church as the body of Christ and the unified ministerial community to the understanding of the Church as centered around its clergy and its monastics.

Before summarizing the Church's history over this thousand-year era—roughly from A.D. 500 to 1500—we will touch briefly on the evolution of western European society, against which the Church can be seen in perspective.

As the period opens, the western and eastern parts of the Roman Empire had been permanently divided for almost one hundred fifty years. The West—far less developed than the East—was largely occupied by barbarians, although Romanized administration and culture survived. The barbarians were either pagans or Arian heretics. Both were hostile to the Christian movement and posed a threat to civilization. It was also during this early period that Mohammed, the founder of the Islam, was born in Mecca (A.D. 570). Though the Moslem religion would remain primarily eastern, its influence would penetrate the West.

This was a thousand-year era of nation building and of the emergence of national identities. Powerful families, banding together in feudal systems, acquired land, wealth, influence, and—ultimately—entire countries. There were sporadic peasant uprisings and plagues. From the late eleventh through the thirteenth centuries there were almost a dozen Crusades—politically and religiously motivated pilgrimages to conquer Moslem lands in the East, to unify Christendom, and to reclaim the Holy Land from the Turks. This entire period was characterized by the rise in power of both the Church *and* the state and the frequent struggles of one or the other to prevail.

Very little is known about the religion of ordinary people in the Dark and Middle Ages. Since we have almost nothing written by laypersons, the little we know about their religious practices comes to us mainly through the monks who wrote about them. What we can infer is that laypersons in general lost access to the culture and the learned traditions of the Church. Language became an important and a discriminating factor. By the eighth century the language of scholarship and worship ceased to be that of everyday speech.[19] Scholarly and liturgical works were written in Latin, and because it was not the vernacular language and ordinary persons were not versed in it, the Church's tradition and scholarship fell beyond the laity's reach. Having lost access to the writing —and thus the thinking—of the Church, the laity could no longer be central to the life of the Christian community.

During the middle of the fourth century the Bishop of Rome came to be considered the successor of St. Peter, Christ's own vicar, the Pope, the head of the Church on earth. The various popes wielded great power, as did the prince-bishops and prince-abbots who accumulated large land holdings and even battled to protect their property. Clergy, in this respect, were no different than other feudal lords. Nonetheless, they were tightly controlled by temporal rulers: "From the sixth century on, the popes had become the pawns of the emperors with their still influential Caesaropopism. . . . Under the incipient feudal system, kings, counts and dukes had priests and even bishops under their control."[20] And until the Second Lateran Council in 1139[21], requiring celibacy of clergy, hereditary episcopacy remained a distinct possibility. The College of Cardinals, the mechanism through which the Pope's authority could be increased and decentralized, was established to police both the clergy and the secular overlords, bringing the Church and its clergy back under the Pope's control.

These developments served to intensify the already wide gulf between laypersons and clergy. The celibacy requirement meant that clergy and laypersons lived very different lifestyles. The institution of the College of Cardinals introduced another clerical stratum into the hierarchy. By the eleventh century one of its functions was the election of popes— totally independent of any lay initiatives whatsoever.[22]

But in many more obvious and immediate ways the Church reminded the laity that they did not matter. Because ordination was absolute, congregations were no longer needed for celebrations of the Holy Eucharist, and as early as the sixth century the saying of private masses became commonplace. When the laity participated, they did so without any sense of equality, for though the presbyter stood at the altar, the people could go no closer than the altar rail where they knelt. The presbyter partook of both bread and wine, but the latter was withheld from the laity.[23] The Council of Constance (1414–1418) gave official validation to the practice of withholding the cup from the laity. When the Bohemian priest John Hus—in many ways Martin Luther's forerunner —disputed this sanction, he was condemned as a heretic and burned at the stake (in 1415).[24] Most of the time, however, the laity merely observed the mass. They received the Sacrament shortly after they had been to confession. About once a year the layperson would privately confess to a presbyter, then receive a single element of the Eucharist. We can hardly imagine that the presbyters, who daily received the Sacrament, also entered the confessional booth as penitents once a day.

The Eucharist was not regarded as the action of the people, but rather of God through the intermediary of the priest. The priest gave his faculties in the service of God. God became present in the midst of the people at the Eucharist. The accent was on the worship of the Lord present in the host. Adoration replaced sharing. . . . They [the people] felt unworthy of so great a God. The fear of God was stronger than the sense of loving partnership. Only the clergy could touch the sacrament. The laity were a sinful mass of people excluded from the sanctuary. . . . The eclipse of the doctrine of the whole church as forming the body of Christ is partly responsible for this individualism and subjectivism. When the oneness and unity of the Church was downgraded, there was no equality for the laity. They did not have a role in the Eucharist. They were nonentities, often not even recipients. They were passive spectators. The laity were preached to and prayed for.[25]

Thus there came to be a double standard of participation in the Holy Eucharist; the very sacrament of unity had become a source of division.

The practice of confessing sins changed through the centuries, too. Confession, which during the patristic age had been public and unusual, now had become a private and precious activity.[26] The private confession became an area of clerical domination and abuse, for along with it came the means by which penitents could pay—literally—for their sins: that is, the whole system of abolishing penalties by the buying of indulgences.[27] The clergy now were no longer simply gatekeepers to the Sacrament, they were gatekeepers who exacted tolls.

Clerical dress became another means of distancing clergy from the people. It made one class of Christians look markedly different than the others. Prior to the fifth century any sort of special attire for clergy was actively discouraged. In A.D. 428 Pope Celestin wrote to the bishops in the south of Gaul, urging them not to introduce special dress, and he warned that the bishop should be distinguished from the people only "by his teaching, not this dress."[28] Nonetheless, clergy took to wearing *long* robes rather than the *short* tunics of ordinary people, and bishops began to wear bright colors (purple and red) that set them visibly apart not only from the laity but from their fellow clergy.[29]

These are just a few of the developments that in effect made the laity subservient and widened the gap between laypersons and clergy in the Dark and Middle Ages. Finally, according to Leclercq,

The change which affected the priesthood at that time was itself the consequence of an even deeper change: one which affected ecclesiology as a whole. Mentalities passed from a conception of the Church, community of Christians, to one which accepted the distance between the lay people and the Church of the clerics. In the first state there was an organic union between pastors and faithful in matters touching liturgical celebrations, councils and other activities of church life. In the second state the idea that predominates is that the whole Christian life and religious state depends upon the priests, their fidelity, the purity of their life and their learning. The different stages of the progressive distancing which took place between the priest and the faithful seems to have arisen from a definition of the Church as consisting mainly of priests.[30]

Throughout the long development of the Christian movement the Church has seldom, if ever, been without its correctives—prophets, reformers, and reform movements calling it back to be itself. Asceticism and monasticism of the fourth century evolved as a response to, and a criticism of, the Christian Church, which had become lax, worldly, and undisciplined. And so with the historical period now under examination. The twelfth and thirteenth centuries saw the revival of heresy and monasticism. Both arose in response to the same cause—corruption— and both were criticisms of the Church.

The most notable heretics were the Albigensians and the Waldensians. The Albigensians came to regard the world and the flesh as evil; their goal was to live a pure life utterly uncluttered by things and people.[31] If their protests were extreme, the Church had gone to extremes to give the Albigensians much to protest against.

Peter Waldo and his so-called heretical movement were less extreme. Waldo came out of the rising merchant class of southern France in the twelfth century. He sold his possessions, gave to the poor, and dedicated himself to a life of poverty. All this would have been quite acceptable to the Church had Waldo kept it at that. But he did not. He read Scripture and taught the Bible to those around him. He began to preach in spite of being (because of his lay status) unauthorized to do so. Church authorities forbade him to preach. Because he would not abide by the official sanction, he and his followers, the Waldensians, were declared heretics.

> At the heart of the Waldensian heresy lay a clear appreciation of the role of the layman in the world as well as in the Church: they lived as paupers in a world of paupers.[32]

Heretics though they may have been considered, the Waldensians still survive today in some parts of Europe, particularly in northern Italy.

The function of heretics in the historical development of Christendom is worth noting because of the service—rarely appreciated at the time—that they render to the Church. Heretics are like prophets and saints. They are like the great political leaders who influence the lives of nations. They emerge at crucial moments to rail against the state of the Church. Their timing is of utmost importance, for the heretic of one age might be the saint of another. According to Kung,

> It is striking that the great heretics rarely took an easy road, they committed themselves *totally* to their ideas, without counting the cost; they subordinated everything to their faith and sacrificed everything to it: this was how they were able to make their tremendous impact. In this the great heretics were very like the great saints. Neither group has ever been understood by lukewarm believers, by shrewd ecclesiastical tacticians and by the diplomats of the Church, great and small, who are not born for martyrdom. . . . Those who boldly and heroically kept faith with their truth, without compromise and without sparing themselves, whose zeal roused whole generations . . . indirectly gave the Church countless creative impulses.[33]

The heretic, unlike the saint, does not submit to the authority of the Church.

Like the heretics, the monastics also corrected the official Church. The great Benedictines, whose celebrated Rule of St. Benedict was the most influential document in the entire history of western monasticism,[34] who Christianized a good deal of northern Europe, who built abbeys that were also great cathedrals—Canterbury, Durham, Winchester, Ely, and Worcester[35]—had lost their pious intensity by the twelfth century. But it had its own corrective: The Cistercians became, in effect, reformed Benedictines. In 1119 William Harding wrote an adaptation of the Benedictine Rule. It revived an austere and rural lifestyle and stressed a rigorous life of prayer. Another reforming offshoot of the Benedictine system was that of the Carthusians, founded by St. Bruno in 1084.

In addition there were the new orders of the twelfth century, chief of which were the Franciscans (founded by St. Francis of Assisi, 1181–1226) and the Dominicans (founded by St. Dominic, c. 1170–1221). Both orders stressed poverty. The Franciscans eliminated everything that would separate them from the poorest members of society: wealth, privileges, fine clothes, comfort, and even books and learning.[36] They lived by the work of their hands and, when necessary, by begging. The Dominicans were an order organized around the practice of preaching throughout Christendom.

Initially the Benedictine order and its reformed off-shoots were lay movements. Only the Dominicans were primarily a clerical order. The monastic orders, and even some of the heretical movements, not only criticized a Church that had turned its back on the people but served as lively alternatives for laypersons who took the responsibilities of the Gospel seriously. The legacy of monastic activity during the Dark and Middle Ages is impressive: service to the poor, schools, hospitals, libraries, cathedrals. Of course even the most idealistic of monastic orders fell short; more and more lay brothers became presbyters, thus compromising the lay character of monasticism, and even the Franciscans, at first so strongly against private ownership, began acquiring property. Be that as it may, monasticism was a viable alternative for some laypersons of the Middle Ages.

All these great religious orders were born out of, and nurtured in, lay surroundings. They were all established in response to the official Church. The Benedictines reacted against the laxity and the clericalism of the Constantinian Church, and Benedictine monks did not ordinarily become priests, and the same with the Carthusians and Cistercians. Francis of Assisi, in the thirteenth century, reacted against the worldly power and influence of the Church and against feudal monasticism by founding an order that was essentially a lay fellowship. However:

> It remains the fact that all these great religious orders in turn, one after the other, have been "clericalized"; this means not only that the majority of their members received ordination as priests but that they have gradually become assimilated to the Church in its most highly institutional form, and have lost contact with the ordinary folk of the Church.[37]

All in all, the Christian Church had been reduced to a mere shadow of what it once was. The full-bodied understanding of the Christian community as the loving fellowship of the priesthood of all believers had been buried under a thousand years of increasing clericalism, excess, corruption, and abuse.

REFORM

In the mid-1400s a layman in Mainz, Germany, discovered a method whereby he could pour hot lead into molds and make letters. Set in rows, these letters could spell words, and rows on rows of words, with ink applied to parchment, could produce pages. Many pages pressed on the same inked trays of letters could produce multiple copies. And the same letters could be moved and rearranged and reused. Think of it: No longer need books be produced by laboriously copying every letter by hand! With the printing press, all sorts of books, religious and otherwise, could be produced in a fraction of the time it once took. With the capability of swiftly printing written materials, more could be produced and more people could be encouraged to learn to read, especially if they were to read the common language they spoke.

Martin Luther has generally been credited with ushering in the Reformation on the eve of All-Saints Day in 1517, when he nailed his "Ninety-five Theses" to the door of the Castle Church in Wittenberg. But perhaps it was another German, the layman Johannes Gutenberg (1400–1468), the inventor of printing, who, because of his revolutionary discovery, made Luther's witness possible. Luther had his "Ninety-five Theses" printed in Latin, intended for a small and learned circle of theologians: "I circulated my disputation notice to academics, inviting them to discuss the issues with me."[38] Within two weeks of its publication, someone had Luther's words translated into German, the language of the people. Copies circulated like wildfire in every direction. The "Theses" sparked instantaneous debate and discussion and tapped into the latent anger at institutional Church abuse that had lain smoldering for generations. To Luther must go the credit, but surely the pent-up outrage would have erupted in time anyway; the availability of printing techniques to produce multiple copies merely hastened the process. So let us not forget our debt to the layman Johannes Gutenberg, father of modern printing and perhaps (indirectly) the grandfather of the Protestant Reformation. And let us also remember the translator—whose identity we do not know—for it was when Luther's words reached the common people that they took on life and vitality for the common good.

Martin Luther, an Augustinian monk and professor of theology, initiated a religious debate, the consequences of which gave birth to a new historical era, an era that would see an end to the Roman Catholic Church's dominance, the creation of reformed (Protestant) Churches, a century and a half of bitter struggle and religious wars, translations of the Bible into the common tongue, and a new understanding of Christian faith.

The Renaissance also saw an explosion of secular learning, the development of a self-consciously secular spirit, the building of universities, the flowering of painting, sculpture, architecture, and music. Brunelleschi, Donatello, Botticelli, Michelangelo, Leonardo da Vinci, Raphael, Titian, Hans Holbein, Pieter Breughel—these artists were the products of their period just as much their works gave the period color, style, beauty, and shape.

Then there were the discoveries and explorations that changed people's thinking about the physical world. The celebrated explorers—Amerigo Vespucci, the Cabots, Cortez, Vasco da Gama, Ferdinand Magellan, and

Christopher Columbus—widened the boundaries of humankind's physical surroundings and possibilities. Columbus believed he could reach the East by sailing west. Although he never got to the East, he did find that the earth is indeed round and that it is small enough to circumnavigate. Just as the explorers widened geographical horizons, the astronomer Nicolaus Copernicus narrowed them in another way. In 1543 he made the revolutionary discovery that the earth revolved around the sun and not the reverse. Since planet Earth could no longer be understood as the center, this changed people's fundamental orientation in the universe.

Knowledge, imagination, creativity, color, artistry, light, expansion and alteration in understanding the physical universe—these were among the gifts of the Renaissance, indications that old ways were being transformed by the new. The foundations of the old world were crumbling; they could no longer hold the emergent civilization. As part of the old giving way to the new, the old Roman Catholic Church—so powerful and yet so diminished by its corruption—could no longer keep its tight hold on its people, who were affected by the Renaissance vitality. Had it not been Martin Luther, it would have been another reformer, for the time was right for drastic changes in official Christendom, as in every other area of human activity.

Though Martin Luther was himself a monk and a presbyter, he directed his attack toward the clergy of the Church of which he was an integral part. With renewed power he revived the New Testament idea of a priesthood of all believers:

> Through baptism all of us are consecrated to the priesthood, as St. Peter says in 1 Peter 2, "Ye are a royal priesthood, a priestly kingdom," and the Book of Revelation says, "Thou hast made us by thy blood to be priests and kings."[39]

Luther also raised an issue that is current today, five hundred years later, in parts of Africa and Latin America. There Christianity is expanding beyond the resources of the churches to staff missions with ordained personnel. Luther described the issue:

> If a little group of pious Christian laymen were taken captive and set down in the wilderness, and had among them no priest consecrated by a bishop, and if there in the wilderness they were to agree in choosing one of themselves, married or unmarried, and were to charge him with the office of baptizing, saying mass, absolving and preaching, such a man would be truly a priest as if all bishops and popes had consecrated him. This is why in cases of necessity anyone can baptize and give absolution, which would be impossible unless we were all priests.[40]

Martin Luther reminded his colleagues of the principle, all but forgotten by the Church hierarchy in the Dark and Middle Ages, that in the
absence of a duly ordained priest, any Christian can do for any other
Christian the things necessary for salvation. Necessity knows no law. The
practice of lay baptism in circumstances of imminent death is as old as
the Christian Church itself. It was given official recognition by the Council
of Elvira in A.D. 306.[41] Laypersons baptizing, laypersons hearing confessions: the Church has never lost sight of these rights, which are affirmed
by most churches' newly revised liturgies.

The Church has been more reluctant to sanction lay presidency at
Eucharist and absolution. Clergy have no "indelible mark," as Luther
called it, no "priestly character," and presbyters do what, in principle,
all Christians can do by virtue of their baptism into the priesthood of
all believers. The presbyter merely holds an office in the Church; if he
ceases to hold that office he reverts to being a layperson. Office is related
to function. Should office cease, so does function.

Absolute ordination—then as now—has been the most important cause
of the continued devaluation of the concept of the priesthood of all
believers and of the place of the laity in the Church. In response to Luther,
the Council of Trent, meeting in 1546, reversed the Council of Chalce-
don's earlier decision and asserted the validity of absolute ordination
because "in the sacrament of orders . . . a character is impressed which
cannot be destroyed or taken away." [42] But Luther carefully marshaled
the biblical evidence (1 Peter 2:5 and 9; Rev. 1:6, 5:10 and 20:6; Gal.
3:28, and John 6:45) for the assertion that all Christians have the same
standing; they are a priesthood entered through baptism and maintained
through faith.[43]

Because all Christians are members of the priesthood, they need no
mediator other than Christ.[44] And because all are equal—regardless of
rank or office—they must have equal access to the bread *and* the wine
of Holy Communion.

> The Sacrament of the Bread [as Luther called the Holy Eucharist]
> must be given in all its entirety to all laymen if they desire it. . . .
> The two kinds constitute one complete sacrament which may not
> be divided. . . . The Sacrament does not belong to the priests, but
> to all men. The priests are not lords, but servants in duty bound
> to administer both kinds to those who desire them, as often as they
> desire them.[45]

Luther stressed the centrality of the sermon. The pulpit, he contended,
was higher than the altar.[46] He put great store in education through

sermons. The sermon is the preacher's means of explaining Scripture, for unless Scripture is understood it cannot come to life in the people. Without the liveliness of the Bible, the Holy Communion itself loses its sacramental quality.[47] The Christian Church, in Luther's view, is the work of the Word, and it is the duty of every Christian, part of the very definition of being Christian, to pass on the Gospel he and she has received.[48] Every Christian is thus a missionary and an evangelist.

This has been a very brief summary of some of Luther's ideas, those he put into practice. In 1522 he translated the New Testament into German, for how could the Word become flesh and dwell among the people unless it could be read and heard in the common tongue? In addition, he compiled a hymnbook for congregational singing, a book that contained thirty-seven texts and some tunes of his own hymns (including his most famous, "A Mighty Fortress Is Our God"). "Worship," he said, "is hearing God's Word and responding in prayer and songs of praise."[49] Finally, he wrote a catechism to help parents and teachers instruct children in the faith.

No other individual since the age of the apostles has had as profound an influence on the development of Christendom as Martin Luther. His reforms led to the development of several Protestant Churches. There was the Evangelical Church in Germany, Luther's church, and Lutheran churches also spread to the Scandinavian countries. In 1523 Ulrich Zwingli brought the movement to Switzerland when he preached at the cathedral in Zurich and began the reform tradition in that country. In 1530 a French preacher named John Calvin experienced a conversion as he was reading Martin Luther's texts. In 1541 he set up a reformed Church in Geneva, Switzerland, guided by the motto "To God Alone Be the Glory."[50] Calvin's Reformed Church spread to the Low Countries, to France, and to Scotland. In France the Calvinists became known as Huguenots, in Scotland, as Presbyterians.[51] In England the reformers never intended to leave the Church of England, only to purify it; thus they became known as Puritans. In 1534 the Act of Supremacy gave birth to the Church of England, a state Church with the English monarch, Henry VIII, as its head.

The Church of England was unique among the Churches that came into being in this period. It was, and is, in effect more a reformed Catholic Church than any of the other strictly Protestant Reformation Churches. The Anglican Church retained more of the features of the old Roman Catholic Church than any of the Evangelical, Lutheran, or Presbyterian Churches. The orders of bishops, presbyters, and deacons, the seven sacraments, and a set liturgy were retained. The Church dropped its allegiance to the Pope as head of the Church and dispensed with the Latin Mass. In time the tradition of clerical celibacy also fell by the wayside.

Also, I would argue that, in practice if not in official Church doctrine, the Anglican Church has retained absolute ordination. In principle, persons were not and are not ordained without a parish in which to exercise their ministry. Evidence abounds, however, to demonstrate that persons are indeed called and empowered by dioceses for ordination with little reference to the prospective ordinand's congregation of origin or other congregation where he or she might exercise presbyterial orders. "Priestcraft," "priestly formation," clergy development, clergy conferences, clergy retreats, rites of ordination to the presbyterate in which bishops and priests lay their hands on the head of the ordinand but exclude lay hands, diocesan priests renewing their ordination vows in the company of each other and the bishop but not among the laypersons among whom they practice their ministries—these ordinary activities of the ordained suggest absolute ordination. It is also expressed in some of the forms of intercessions of the Episcopal *Book of Common Prayer*. For example, in Form II of the Prayers of the People the worshipper prays "for all ministers and people,"[52] as if clergy were not people and laypersons were not ministers.

> Expressions such as "ministers and people," though commonly used, must be reckoned unfortunate, for they obscure the fact that the ministers themselves belong to the people of God, and that the whole people has a ministry.[53]

But most of all, because ordination is for life, whether or not the presbyter has a ministry in a congregation, that ministry is absolute.

This issue aside: The Anglican Church that evolved during the Reformation was both a reformed Catholic Church and a Protestant Church.

BEYOND THE REFORMATION

Because this chapter is a history of the Church's clericalization rather than of the laity's accomplishments, there is much less to say about the period after the Reformation. The Reformation rediscovered the early Church idea of the ministerial community as the priesthood of all believers. Great changes occurred throughout the entire Christian world as a result. The laity were indeed rediscovered, and Christianity has never been as distorted as it was in the Dark and Middle Ages. New Protestant denominations, which took the ministry of the body seriously, were established and have flourished.

The Quaker Movement—with *no* ordained clergy—came about through the initiative of George Fox in the 1640s. The modern missionary movement was essentially lay. Count Zinzendorf—initially a layman—set the Moravian Church on its missionary course with a small group of laypersons who carried the Gospel to such places as the Caribbean. Puritanism was primarily lay-centered in the Plymouth Colony. Until the arrival of the first ordained minister, Elder Brewster served as both the political leader and the leader of the religious community.[54] And the Baptist Movement, with roots in the Congregationalist tradition, was also very much lay.

> The typical Baptist preacher of the early [American] frontier came from the ranks of the people, among whom he lived and worked. He was a farmer and worked on the land five or six days a week, except when he was called upon to hold weekday meetings or funerals.[55]

The Disciples of Christ, originating in the early 1800s, was a lay-centered Church. Methodism was primarily a lay movement with origins in the Anglican Church. It relied for its expansion on traveling preachers and lay teachers.

The midnineteenth century saw various lay-initiated movements: The Young Men's Christian Association (Y.M.C.A.), "seeking to unite those young men who desire to associate their efforts for the extension of His [Jesus Christ's] Kingdom among men," was formed in the 1860s. It was followed by the Y.W.C.A. several years later.[56] Leaders in the antislavery movement were Christians representing a variety of denominations.

Overcrowding, unsafe working conditions, abuse of child factory workers, unsanitary living places, ruthless bosses—these ills contributed to the social ferment that gave rise to a new breed of urban social reformers. The Settlement House Movement established University Settlement in New York (1886), Hull House in Chicago (1889), Andover House —later called South End Settlement—in Boston (1891). The American Boy Scouts (1910) and the Girl Scouts (1912)[57] were part of the same philanthropic thrust. There were reformers of prisons, reformers who sought improvements in the care and treatment of the mentally ill. A few of them were: Dorothea Dix, Stanton Coit, Charles Stover, Jane Addams, and Clifford Beers. Then there were the journalists and writers who brought poor social conditions to the public's attention—such people as Lincoln Steffens *(The Shame of the Cities),* Jacob Riis *(How the Other Half Lives: Studies Among the Tenements of New York),* Upton Sinclair *(The Jungle),* and Ida Tarbell *(The History of Standard Oil).*[58] There were also unionizers and labor reformers.

The turn of the nineteenth century into the twentieth was, in every way, a reform era. It can safely be assumed that the reformers were motivated by something more than humanitarian impulses. One could even consider them "religious," for they carried on their reformations with energy and missionary zeal. With the exception of Dorothea Dix's writings, conspicuously absent in the records they left is any mention of religious motivation. Nowhere is there anything to suggest specifically that the reformers went about their work as a result of their commitment to Christ and his ministry of salvation in the world. One wonders why. Hans-Rudi Weber, writing about the rediscovery of the laity in the Ecumenical Movement in the 1930s, said:

> The process of industrialization and secularization which tend to edge the Church out of daily life into a religious ghetto; the fact [is] that the Church is becoming almost everywhere a minority which has great difficulty communicating with the modern world.[59]

Perhaps it had begun to dawn on Church leaders that the laity had gone into areas of human concern consciously without the Church to satisfy their humanitarian inclinations. At any rate, in 1937 J.H. Oldham, in a preparatory volume for the Oxford Conference (a forerunner of the World Council of Churches) on "Church, Community and State" wrote:

> In relation to issues which will come before the Oxford Conference, nothing could be plainer than that if the Christian is in the present and future to bring about changes . . . in the thought, habits and practice of society, it can only do this through being the living, working faith of multitudes of lay men and women conducting the ordinary affairs of life. . . . If the Church is to be an effective force in the social and political sphere, our first task is to laicize our thought about it.[60]

The First Assembly of the World Council of Churches, meeting in Amsterdam in 1948, appointed a committee to explore the "significance of the laity in the Church."[61] Lay issues have continued to be on World Council agendas ever since.

After all is said and done, the Church is still clericalized. Perhaps not as clericalized as it was, but still clericalized nonetheless.

Martin Luther stressed the importance of the congregation, but Lutheran pastors ultimately became dominant. Luther's ideals were largely just that—ideals. Lutheran Churches, then and now, are far less the communities of the priesthood of all believers than the parishes of other denominations (e.g., the Baptists). Some American Pentecostalist Churches probably come nearer to the New Testament idea of a priesthood of all believers than the major Protestant denominations. John Wesley—despite his reliance on lay preachers—never allowed lay presidency at Eucharist in Methodist Churches. And very shortly after Methodism's establishment as an independent denomination in the U.S.A. in 1784, its superintendents came to be known as bishops.

The Second Vatican Council, meeting from 1963 to 1965, un-questionably brought about sweeping changes in the Roman Catholic Churches: altars were pulled away from the walls, mass in the vernacular, Holy Communion with both bread and wine for all members of the congregation, a whole new emphasis was placed on the laity in the community of faith. But mono-sexual, celibate clergy have been retained. The Episcopal Church recovered much of the early Church's liturgical practice through the reform that yielded the 1979 *Book of Common Prayer.* Lutherans and some of the other Protestant denominations revised their liturgies also.

With such major liturgical changes, can we now say that the ancient role of the laity has been recovered and that the ministerial community of the priesthood of all believers has been restored? Yes and no.

Yes: Certainly the framework of the revised liturgies allows for far greater lay participation in congregational worship than has been known for hundreds of years. Laypersons can do much more than they generally think. Many strong lay leaders in all denominations have pointed out the multitude of ways laypersons can take hold of their God-given ministries and express them within present institutional structures.

No: The reformers did not go far enough. As long as the Church acknowledges absolute ordination and such features as "priestly character" rather than "Christian character" as long as lay ministry is interpreted as primarily serving the Church in the Church; as long as churches con-tinue to be congregations gathered around presbyters (who exercise power and control) rather than unified and equal ministerial communities that engage and affirm the ministries of all members; until models of spirituality appropriate to the whole people of God—as distinct from ascetics as models that appeal to an elite few—are adopted; and until laypersons write their own authentic theology, the Church will remain clericalized.

Reform of ordained ministry must proceed alongside the reform and recovery of the ministry of the laity. But though both ministries must change, laypersons must take the initiative in making the reforms. Finally, according to Jan Grootaers, it will take the remainder of the twentieth century to

Move towards this balance of revising the status of laity within the institutional Church. . . . One part of the Church can never move forward without the other, for both are subject, in common obedience, to one and the same Lord.[62]

So let the reformation proceed . . .

CHAPTER 5

A THEOLOGY OF THE LAITY
BY THE LAITY

All who are inspired and uplifted by the Spirit of Christ
are in posession of the true theology, though they be
only ditch diggers or weavers.

—Erasmus, 1516

Whenever people reflect on God's act of revelation, they are engaged in the process of theology; whenever they move into the area of reflection the interpretation, they enter into the realm of theology.

John Macquarrie has said,

Theology may be considered as the most sophisticated kind of meditation, for it is the reflective attempt to understand as fully as possible and to assimilate the meaning of the Christian religion.[1]

And Gustavo Gutiérrez is quoted as saying:

A Christian is defined as a follower of Jesus, and reflection on the experience of following constitutes the central theme of any solid theology.[2]

Here two very different theologians—John Macquarrie, a British Anglican, and Gustavo Gutiérrez, a South American liberation theologian —define theology. Both are agreed that it is reflection. This chapter deals with theology, whereas the next four chapters will consider various aspects of spirituality. Let us be clear at the outset about what we mean by these terms: *Theology* is reflection. It is reflection on the nature of God's revelation to persons and the meaning and interpretation of such revelation. It is, as Macquarrie said, a type of meditation. Christian *spirituality,* on the other hand, is following Jesus, following him wherever he is to be found—in creation, in communities, in social and political institutions, in persons.

The starting point of any engagement in theology is revelation through faith, God revealing himself in the lives of the faithful as they engage in their myriad activities in the world. This faith, as Francisco José Moreno has pointed out, is not necessarily the result of rational inquiry, but "once faith is established, then we resort to reason to defend it."[3]

Theology begins where people are. As the nonordained, priestly people of God living out their Christian lives in the workplace and the marketplace, in supermarkets, in service stations, in factories and schools and hospitals, in homes and neighborhoods, a liberated laity urgently needs to reflect on Christian living and being and believing so they will be able to interpret for themselves the ancient yet ever-contemporary biblical themes of life/death, alienation/commitment, sin/salvation, skepticism/belief, hope/despair, wealth/poverty. Laypersons need not look far for the raw material of their theology; their own lives—where they have their being and livelihoods—are enough. They need only reflect on what they are doing and incorporate those experiences into their living faith. Then they will, in the very broadest sense, be engaged in the theological enterprise. As Richard Mouw, an American layman, has said:

> We need to develop a theology of and for the laity that is a non-elitist theology. I think a non-elitist theology of and for the laity has to develop a real theology for waiters and waitresses and florists, and for people who work in clothing stores, and people who work in grocery stores at the check-out lanes and in the lettuce rooms, and for housewives.[4]

Theology cannot be written once and for all time. It is a continuous and dynamic process, for God is continually revealing himself to his people. Furthermore, in the theological engagement the theologian himself or herself develops, through his or her work and the ongoing experience of living and believing. The modern artist Barnett Newmann, in reference to his series of paintings "Stations of the Cross," said, "It is as I work that the work begins to have an effect on me. Just as I affect the canvas, so does the canvas affect me."[5] Theology is in a constant state of flux because theologians live, mature, and develop as they "grow into the fullness of Christ." And because society is not static and theology is, in part, dependent on, and related to, it, the latter has to be written and rewritten to interpret belief continually in light of the present. Reflection, interpretation, and reinterpretation—this is a fluid process, this is theology.

As in the historical clericalization of the Church, theology has been taken out of the hands of the ordinary people of God. Since as early as the fourth century, theology has been the work of the Church's ordained scholars. These professional Christians have interpreted the faith for each other and have assumed they were doing so for the laity. Indeed, our understanding of the Church was, and still is, dependent on them. Perhaps this is why the laity have, in reality, understood so little.

> There has grown up an inflated theological jargon. . . . It is disastrous for the Church when theology becomes purely an academic study and is divorced from the everyday life of the Christian community in the world.[6]

Certainly professional, academic theologians will continue to write for each other, and some of their work will be helpful to some laypersons. But the laity must now begin to write their own theology, a theology that will bring to expression their life as the people of God engaged in the daily routine of God's world. The time is ripe, for the laity are indeed just beginning to rediscover their identity in the Christian community. And when a people begins to draw together and develop a collective identity two things usually happen: (1) they begin to recover their history; and (2) they write a history drawn from, and reflective of, their experience as a people.

This process, resulting from an awakened identity, is clearly illustrated in the emergent self-consciousness of American blacks. Martin Luther King started American blacks on a journey of self-discovery, a journey to learn in fresh ways what it means to be a people in this time and place. The identity question—*Who am I?*—is quickly followed by the historical question—*Where did I come from?* Alex Haley, the author of *Roots,* helped a whole generation of people reclaim their history. James Cone and C. Eric Lincoln are among the black theologians who have interpreted that history through their theologies of black liberation. Their work has not stopped there, nor has it only affected black Americans. The journey toward the liberation of black persons, the untapping of their history and the writing of an authentic black theology have ultimately and profoundly affected all Americans' understanding of the participation of *all* citizens in public life.

So must it be with the laity of the Church, as they more and more reflect on the meaning of God's revelation to them in their day-to-day lives. For the professional clerical theologians of the Church to continue to write a universal theology is no longer appropriate, if in fact it ever was. They cannot write a theology for the laity for the same reason white persons cannot write black theology; no one can write with any degree of authenticity about others' experience.

A theology of the laity, by the laity, and for the laity is not to be understood as a mere academic exercise. Nor ought it to be understood as a watered-down, easy version of academic theology. Nor as a frill or a luxury.

> Theology, properly understood, is no luxury. It is *a necessity* if there is to be a true people of God. Theology is the people's understanding of its own *raison d'etre,* and without such an understanding, there is not a people but only an uncertain, drifting, spineless mass of human beings. If the Church sometimes appears to be such a jellylike mass, one reason for this is the lack of any clear theological understanding. To supply this understanding is the business of a theology for the people, a theology which will not be the specialized preserve of scholars and professionals but which will relate to the interests and life situations of the great bulk of Christians. . . . There has been too much neglect in building up the whole people in theological understanding.[7]

What is needed, according to Richard Mouw, is a "contextualized theology," one that arises out of daily life and experience. As Mouw pointed out, all theology is "contextualized," whether it be white, Anglo-Saxon theology, black theology, Hispanic theology, or any others.[8] A theology arises out of lived faith; it becomes an integral part of the liberation of a people. As the laity more and more liberate themselves to be the Church in the world, the more it will become necessary for them to write their own theology.

> We've got to take the practical questions and answers of our neighbors and try to match them up with questions and answers of the word of God. The resulting theology will be a contextualized theology. . . . There is a sense where we are sandwiched between the word of God as it has been understood in a clergy-dominated church, and the actual reality of the laity in the world. We have to bring the experiences and the questions of the laity to the word of God for illumination and for answers. Then the laity must, in turn, take their understanding of God and again exegete [*sic,* i.e., explain] it, while at the same time exegeting the *actual culture in which they participate*—the insurance office, or the bank, or the grocery store or the restaurant.[9]

From the troubled land of South Africa has emerged an example of the contextualized theology I believe is needed in North America today. There, during July and August 1985, an ecumenical working committee of lay and ordained Church leaders met to reflect on Christianity in relationship to the political crisis in their country:

As the crisis was intensifying in the country, as more and more people were killed, maimed and imprisoned, as one black township after another revolted against the apartheid regime, as the people refused to be oppressed or to cooperate with oppressors, facing death by the day, and as the apartheid army moved into the townships to rule by the barrel of the gun, a number of theologians who were concerned about the situation expressed the need to reflect on this situation to determine what response by the Church and by all Christians in South Africa would be most appropriate.[10]

The result of the committee's reflections was *The Kairos Document,* published in September 1985. It was also called *Challenge to the Church: A Theological Comment on the Political Crisis in South Africa.* It was signed by a widely representative group of one hundred fifty Christians and, in their words, was "not intended as a final statement of the truth but as *the direction God is leading us at this moment in our history* [italics mine]."[11] Though there are not many similarities between the United States and South Africa, the American laity have much to learn from the *Kairos* theological engagement.

How is the legitimacy of any theology tested? The acid test is a positive response to these questions: Is it rooted in the concrete experiences of the people? Does it ring true? Does it encourage the pursuit of justice? Does it nurture faith? According to Leonardo Boff:

The ultimate criterion determining the truth of any and all theology is whether it produces a life of faith, hope, and charity. Theology is true insofar as it is translated into meditation, prayer, conversion, the following of Christ, and commitment to our fellow human beings.[12]

Boff is not suggesting that all laypersons become, in the formal sense, theologians. Certainly all laypersons ought to think theologically, but not every Christian will become a theologian, just as not every clergyperson is a theologian. But some laypersons will give expression to the theological experiences of the laity as a whole. They will be theologians in every sense of the word.

In the final analysis, the Church speaks and acts on the world through her laity, who are part of the world. The laity can only speak and act effectively from the basis of a solid theology—one that is of the laity, by the laity, and for the world.

CHAPTER 6

FOLLOWING JESUS

I thought I could acquire faith by trying to live a holy
life. Later I discovered that it is only by living completely in this world that one learns to believe.
—Dietrich Bonhoeffer,
Letters and Papers from Prison

There is no fancy way to define Christian spirituality. It is, simply,
following Jesus. It is being a disciple of Jesus. "Spirituality is the style
of a person's response to Christ before the challenge of everyday life,
in a given historical and cultural environment."[1] Gustavo Gutiérrez has
likened it to a journey, a community on a journey. He does not ignore
the personal dimension; rather, he sees the individual journey as part of
the whole journey of the people of faith.[2]

> Spirituality is not restricted to the so-called religious aspects of life:
> prayer and worship. It is not limited to one sector but is all-
> embracing, because the whole of human life, personal and com-
> munal, is involved in the journey. A spirituality is a manner of life
> that gives profound unity to our prayer, thought and action.[3]

Dietrich Bonhoeffer, the courageous Lutheran pastor and theologian who
had written about spirituality (in *The Cost of Discipleship*) before participating in the resistance movement in Nazi Germany, wrote again about
the spiritual journey—this time from prison, some ten months before
being executed. (He did not think he had expressed the meaning of
spirituality adequately in his previous book.) In his cell, he reflected, "I
thought I could acquire faith by trying to live a holy life. Later I discovered
that it is only by living completely in this world that one learns to
believe."[4] He explained:

> Man is challenged to participate in the sufferings of God. . . . He
> must live a "wordly" life and so participate in the suffering of
> God. . . . To be a Christian does not mean to be religious in a

particular way, to cultivate some particular form of ascetism (as a sinner, a penitent or a saint), but to be a man. It is not some religious act which makes a Christian what he is, but participation in the life of the world . . . allowing oneself to be caught up in the way of Christ. . . .[5]

Spirituality is following Christ. It is up to Christians in every age and place to ask themselves how and where they follow Christ. How is Christ to be followed? Where is he to be followed? Congregations, communities of faith, must give tangible meaning and expression in action to what exactly it means to be a people who follow Christ, a people whose spiritual journey becomes Christ's journey through his people.

Following Jesus is the way—the *only* way, Christians believe—to ultimate meaning, purpose, peace, justice, happiness, liberation. "I am the way, the truth, and the life" (John 14:6).

Where is Christ to be followed? The starting place for the spiritual journey is the same as the starting place for an authentic theology (described in the previous chapter). "You, O Lord, are in the midst of us and we are called by your name" (Jer. 14:9). We follow Jesus where we are, for wherever we are, so he is. We begin the journey by looking around us, by looking at the ways Christ is already at work in our families, our friends, our neighbors, our communities, and our workplaces. We might recognize what is there already and see it as a gift, a given, God's given gift.

The first objective of the Maryknoll Society, stated by the General Chapter in 1979, expresses well this factor of recognition as integral to following Jesus: "To recognize and elaborate a mission of spirituality which integrates community, prayer, a simple life-style, apostolic work, and commitment to the poor."[6] An authentic spirituality is not a labored or artificial straining to meet Christ; Christ is with us already. Seeking Christ is opening our eyes to and in the world where Christ is already acting in the lives of persons and in social groups. Recognizing and then, to borrow the Maryknollers' word, "elaborating." Elaborating is naming, bringing to light that spirituality which we see with our eyes, understand with our minds, and believe with our hearts. The spiritual journey begins precisely where we are, in recognizing Christ in those around us and in elaborating—or appropriating—the life of Christ thus revealed. This is the spiritual way: a discipleship to which all persons have access, for it is right here in our midst.

How sad it is that even life's best gifts become, in time, distorted and corrupted. Throughout history, selfishness has reared its ugly head, again and again, to hoard for a few what ought to be for the many. Corruption is always with us; it always has been, and historical hindsight tells us nothing is ever once and for all time reformed. Protestantism did not get rid of clericalism, the Reformation did not eliminate individualistic piety, and the Oxford Movement was not ultimately successful in linking sacrament and social service.[7]

Retreats, quiet days, studying the works of medieval ascetics, the desert fathers, and contemporary spiritual gurus are enjoying great popularity today. One can get some satisfaction from these activities. But after all is said and done, the traditional spiritual journey—and its present-day counterpart—has, by and large, become privatized and individualized; it has become elitist and may inhibit social action. Louis Weil, liturgist and historian of the Oxford Movement, remarked that,

> The separation today between piety and action seems as great
> as ever, and is one of the most urgent problems which a renewed
> liturgical theology must address.[8]

In North America the traditional spiritual journey has, in many ways, come to be "my journey," "my interior life," "my spiritual direction," to be directed toward individual rather than broadly humanitarian values, with the goal of personal perfection. It is frequently characterized by insensitivity to needs of the real, concrete persons who surround Christians as they follow the spiritual way.[9]

> Individualism and spiritualism thus combine to impoverish and
> even distort the following of Jesus. An individualistic spirituality
> is incapable of offering guidance in this following to those who
> are on a collective enterprise. . . . Nor does it do justice to the
> different dimensions of the human person.[10]

The spiritual journey has become elitist: Spirituality, as we have generally come to understand it, is an elitist, introspective, often intellectualized activity, geared to a minority of Christians but held up as an ideal for all. The pursuit of the spiritual journey traditionally involves retreats, quiet days, time away, spiritual directors, specialized reading. By their nature, these are exclusive activities best suited for those who have the leisure, the money, and the mastery of their work and family schedules to allow their participation.

> Most retreat experiences are expensive, non-lay luxuries, and are
> at best modified versions of experiences in the lives of religious.[11]

If the layperson attends a retreat at a monastary or a convent, he or she will probably be impressed by the quiet and solitude of the surroundings and even by the holiness of the retreat leader. Invariably the layperson will consider him- or herself, by comparison, in a negative or inferior light. Rarely will it occur to the lay visitor that the monastic retreat leader, unlike him- or herself, is free of such material worries as job, children, spouse, food, and shelter and, thus unencumbered, is free to contemplate the holy.

> It is rather difficult to face up to the fact that the minorities [who exercise spirituality in monastic life] are privileged minorities from the social, cultural, and, to some extent, economic standpoint.[12]

The point about retreats and quiet days patterned after monastic spirituality is not that there is anything wrong with them as such but that they suggest a model and an ideal for lay spirituality.

Finally, traditional spirituality may inhibit Christian social action. The following of Christ, the quest for holiness, can very easily become a substitute for representing Christ in social action. W.H. Auden is quoted as saying:

> As the records of the mystics show, the great temptation of the contemplative life—many of them passed through periods when they succumbed to it—is some form or other of Quietism, an indifference to and an impatience with, not only "works" in the conventional sense, but also all the institutional and intellectual aspects of human life.[13]

And according to Leonardo Boff:

> We must break out of the circle of self-absorption and pay heed to the bloodied face of our fellow human beings. For they are the great sacrament of God, the signs and instruments of authentic divine reality. If we do not share life with the oppressed, we do not share life with God.[14]

The following of Jesus that issues in action is not a new idea; it is as old as Christendom itself. Few have stated the case better than one of the key figures of the Oxford movement, E.B. Pusey. In 1852, in a sermon titled "God With Us," he said:

> Real love to Christ must issue in love to all who are Christ's, and real love to Christ's poor must issue in self-denying acts of love towards them . . . seeing Christ in the poor, the sick, the hungry, the thirsty, the naked, we must . . . seek them out as we would seek Christ, looking for a blessing from it. . . . It was promised of old time, as a blessing, "The poor shall never cease out of the land," and now we know the mercy of this mysterious blessing, for they are the presence of our Lord.[15]

Prayer prepares the path for the spiritual journey, and the Gospels are full of innumerable accounts of Jesus at prayer (Matt. 26:36–44; Mark 1:35–36, 6:31–32; Luke 3:21, 5:16, 9:18 and 28, 11:1–2, 22:32, 39–45; and John 17). Jesus had the habit of slipping away quietly and un-announced to pray, and he invariably left his disciples wondering where he was and what he was doing. In studying the characteristics of Jesus' prayers, one notes that they were *always* related to concrete action. (Jesus never prayed when action did not follow.) His prayers also afforded him discernment of the way, closeness with the Father, knowledge and comfort, but action was the principal consequence. And the more Christ was steeped in the world of action, the more he prayed.

At the same time it must be recognized that Jesus *said* very little about prayer as a way of discipleship. He gave his disciples certain guidelines to follow when they prayed (Matt. 6:5–8), and he taught them the Lord's Prayer (Matt. 6:9–13, Luke 11:2–4). In Luke's account it is not even Jesus who first broached the subject of prayer; it was one of the disciples: "Lord, teach us to pray, just as John taught his disciples" (Luke 11:1). Moreover, Jesus stressed that the true test of discipleship lies not in words: "It is not those who say 'Lord, Lord,' who will enter the kingdom, but the person who does the will of my father who is in heaven" (Matt. 7:21–22).

Prayer cannot take the place of action; action must follow prayer. Dag Hammarskjöld, the Swedish layman who became secretary-general of the United Nations, stated in a simple and straightforward way what ought to be the action-oriented focus of the spiritual journey: "In our era, the road to holiness necessarily passes through the world of action."[16]

The original title of this chapter was "Toward a Lay Spirituality." It was chosen because I felt it was important to paint, in strokes as broad as possible, the Church's urgent need for a way of following Jesus that was not dictated by the clerical minority and, in the absence of any authentic spirituality appropriate for the lay majority, to point to avenues that would lead to such a lay spirituality. The title was an acknowledge-ment that there was, therefore, a distinctive clerical spirituality. Living with the title and having read the sources on spirituality (and particularly on clerical spirituality) and having thought through the issues of spirituality, I am now convinced that there is, in fact, *no distinctive spirituality for the ordained that would not also be appropriate for laypersons.*

As Schillebeeckx pointed out in *The Church with a Human Face,* "priestly spirituality" was, in effect, an invention of the Middle Ages, conceived for the minority of presbyters, who were also monastics. It was never intended for those occupied in pastoral care (which, of course, was the majority of the ordained).[17] Even for Josse Clichtove (1472–1543), who, one might say, brought the clericalization of the Church to new heights, "priestly spirituality" was only intended for "mass priests," for the numerous presbyters ordained at the beginning of the sixteenth century without any pastoral responsibility. Clichtove

> wanted a new spirituality of the priesthood, but on the basis of a very narrow theological view of the Church's ministry (which is not really a ministry but simply a state). Unfortunately he cast this already one-sided spirituality in juridical forms. Also, above all under his influence, the Catholic image of the priest came to be seen in the light of an absolutizing of the law, for which the mediaeval image of the priest had laid only a very few foundations. . . . The image of the priest as the solitary reader of "masses" without further pastoral responsibilities, took on a certain divine aura.[18]

It is only in the twentieth century, according to Schillebeeckx, that voices have been raised to apply the notion of "priestly spirituality" to the diocesan priests involved in parish work.[19] We know, too, that "priestly spirituality" became a major feature among Anglicans in the Oxford Movement of the nineteenth century.

Any distinctions between a lay spirituality and an ordained person's spirituality are artificial. John Robinson would agree, for he is quoted as saying:

> I am not convinced that there is more than a difference of degree between the "secular" spirituality which is appropriate to the clergy and to the laity. I believe the yearning which is felt for something more "earthed" reflects a more general discontent with the traditional types of spirituality and that we clergy cover up the uncomfortable knowledge that they have long been failing us, and that we have failed to communicate a relevant spirituality to our people, by saying that what we need is something new for "the laity."[20]

Following Jesus is, simply, following Jesus. There is no special way for the clergy to follow Jesus, just as there is no special way the laity ought to follow him. There may be some difference in emphasis because clerical ministries are based mainly within the institutional Church and the world is the arena for the ministry of the laity, but generally speaking, following Jesus is following Jesus, period. Properly conceived, the spirituality suitable for the clergy is also appropriate for the laity and vice versa. To continue to suggest there is a distinct clerical spirituality will only serve

to perpetuate the division between lay and ordained Christians and further
fragment the ministerial community, in which all are to share in Christ's
priesthood.

> A great confidence and joy abounds as one meets and loves God
> in the streets or at home as well as at the altar, a joy which gives
> substance to one's capacity to be a priestly person, a walking sign
> of Emmanuel—God with us. This is the priest's prayer without
> ceasing, being that sign.
>
> The cardinal image of priestly spirituality is the servant Lord
> dying on the Cross, with the people on his heart. At the foot of
> the Cross is another image, that of the Blessed Mother, not dis-
> placing her Son, but, by long tradition, a symbol for the contempla-
> tion of other aspects of the mystery of the Incarnation. Mary is also
> a paradigm for priestly spirituality, especially for this grace to say
> yes to God in the world and bear it, and pray without ceasing
> over it.[21]

This quotation was excerpted from an essay entitled "Priestly Spirituality," and it is clear its author meant a spirituality for the ordained. The
spirituality it describes would, however, be more appropriate for laity
and ordained alike, for all God's priestly people.

How ought all Christians to follow Jesus in ways neither privatized
nor individualized and elitist, in ways that encourage social action and,
even more, social transformation?

A spirituality for our time will be encouraged by the saints, those
models of discipleship whose lives and examples can teach us how to
follow Christ with courage and imagination. It will be rooted in the soil
of everyday existence while nurturing the affairs of everyday life. A
spirituality for our day will seek and find and follow Christ through social
action, pointing the way to social transformation.

> Pious human beings will always ask:
> Where do we find God?
> Religions mark out the main places and the privileged
>   situations in which we encounter God:
> e.g., prayer, the interior life,
> a lifestyle of simplicity and asceticism,
> and unselfish service to our fellow human beings.
> Christians know that they encounter God in the Church,
> in its sacraments, in the sacred words of Scripture,
> and in fraternal, loving encounter with their neighbors.
> The question is legitimate and the answers relevant.
> But we learn from Jesus that the truly basic question is

a different one:

i.e., Where does God himself want to be encountered by human beings?[22]

Where indeed does God choose to be encountered by human beings?

CHAPTER 7

RUNNING WITH THE SAINTS

Since we are surrounded by so great a cloud of witnesses . . . let us run with perseverance the race that
is set before us.

—Hebrews 12:1–2

Where does God want to be encountered by human beings? How is Christ
to be encountered? We know only too well that a spiritual journey led
Christ to the Cross, and ever since his crucifixion the road traveled by
his followers has been drenched with the blood of martyrs, known and
unknown. Countless men and women in every age have run Christ's race,
they have persevered, and they are now numbered in that great cloud
of witnesses. These saints are like a gigantic heavenly cheering section,
urging us to continue Christ's race with courage, willingness to risk, joy,
and imagination.

THE CHURCHES' MODELS FOR DISCIPLESHIP

How fortunate it is that we, still on our earthly pilgrimage, are nurtured
on the way by that great cloud of witnesses, men and women who
followed Christ in their time, holy persons whose lives and examples
encourage us. A few of these holy persons have been memorialized in
the liturgical Churches' calendars of saints. Those included in the Roman
Catholic, Episcopal, and Lutheran calendars. They are, as it were, those
churches' superheroes. By learning about their lives and praying their
prayers we too may come to know Christ. We learn how to serve Christ
by identifying with those who have, in their lives, illustrated the true and
often costly meaning of discipleship. St. Ignatius of Loyola is said to have
been converted by reading the lives of the saints. Now he is commemorated in the Roman Catholic calendar, and by remembering his

life, others too may be converted and become disciples. By observing the saints' days throughout the Christian year we recall the godly persons who have gone before us and at the same time have the opportunity of imitating their living and believing in our day.

Everyone has his or her favorite saints in the denominational calendars. A few favorites of mine are: Mary, the Apostle Paul, Martin Luther, Martin Luther King, Jr., Dietrich Bonhoeffer, and St. Francis of Assisi.

When I was too young to know the meaning of the words, my mother taught me St. Francis's prayer "Lord, make us instruments of your peace. . . ." Now I know the words' meaning, and I am uneasy because I fall so short of the ideal it expresses. Is there a mother for whom Mary, mother of our Lord, is not a special saint? Every mother is a bearer of life, a bearer of the mystery and the wonder of creation; every mother suffers twice—once when her child suffers, once for herself. Having watched nightlong over children with high fevers, I have felt Mary has been my companion in the still hours before the dawn. Having borne children once, mothers continue to bear with them all the rest of their lives—just like Mary.

> When we look at the lives of those who have faithfully followed Christ, we are inspired with a new reason for seeking the city which is to come. At the same time we are shown a most safe path by which, among the vicissitudes of the world and in keeping with the state of life and condition proper to each of us, we will arrive at perfect union with Christ, that is, holiness.[1]

Considered another way, the official calendars of saints testify to the utter failure of the laity's religious life.

> If saints are our models of success, than the lay life seems a spiritual failure when judged by canonization statistics. . . . The small numbers of canonized lay saints may be due in large part to the fact that lay persons have no effective way of lobbying. . . . This ecclesiastically dispensed spirituality is an unhealthy form of spiritual discrimination. After two thousand years, where are the lay saints canonized for their integration of Christianity and work, or of prayer and politics? Who are the lay models of conjugal love, of family life, of civic service?[2]

Eighty-one percent of the saints in the Roman Catholic calendar are clerical or monastic.[3] Similarly, 83 percent of the saints in the Episcopal Church's calendar are monastics or ordained persons. Inasmuch as these calendars can be equated with institutional recognition of models of discipleship, monastics and priests are *the* models and bishops the models *par excellence.* One hundred deacons, bishops, presbyters, archbishops and monastics are recognized in the Episcopal calendar; over half that number (fifty-nine) are bishops and archbishops. Of the 17 percent of the laity commemorated, four are royalty—hardly models with which ordinary Christians can identify.[4] Furthermore, the Episcopal calendar does not honor so much as one American layperson. As of this writing, the Episcopal Church's Standing Liturgical Commission has published eight new names to present to the 1985 General Convention for inclusion in the calendar: three are monastics, one a deacon, four laypersons (who include three kings and a queen).[5] At last two American laypersons are being proposed, and they are King Kamehameha and Queen Emma of Hawaii—hardly persons with whom one can easily identify. What is the meaning of such blatant exclusion of laypersons? Reviewing the over two hundred years of American experience, the Episcopal Church cannot find even one layperson—other than a king and a queen, that is—who would make a worthy addition to its calendar of saints? There could scarcely be a more revealing indication—or a more stunning indictment—of how the Episcopal Church truly regards the lives and witness of her laity.

None of the above is intended as a criticism of the heroic persons—including King Kamehameha and Queen Emma—whom the Church has seen fit to commemorate; many of them were martyred for their discipleship, and that is no small achievement. It is, rather, the one-sidedness of the calendars, so heavily weighted with monastics and clerics, that is being attacked.

Before leaving the Roman Catholic and Episcopal calendars, one other criticism must be noted: These Churches only memórialize persons of their own denominations. Saints from before the split of Eastern and Western Christendom in 1054 are listed on both calendars. Since then the Roman Catholic Church has memorialized, on its official calendar, exclusively Roman Catholics. The Episcopal Church, in its official calendar, has commemorated only Anglicans and Episcopalians!

The Lutheran calendar, as found in the 1978 *Lutheran Book of Worship,* is better as far as its ecumenicity as well as its catholicity are concerned. The Lutheran calendar includes George Fox, founder of the Quaker movement, and John Hus, a reformer considered a heretic by some. Martin Luther King, Jr., is there, as well as Nicolaus Copernicus, the astronomer, and Albrecht Dürer, the artist. And considering the Lutheran Church's antipapal beginnings, it is remarkable that the calendar includes a pope, albeit a recent and reforming one—John XXIII. But however preferable the Lutheran calendar may be to its Roman Catholic and Episcopal counterparts, it is still more clericalized than one would have expected, 62 percent of the inclusions being pastors/presbyters, bishops and archbishops, monastics, and a deacon and a deaconness.[6]

Considering the outright exclusion of all but a small number of laypersons from the Episcopal and Roman Catholic calendars of saints, an exclusion that has been practiced for hundreds of years, it is quite remarkable that it has taken until now for us to question the appropriateness of our modes and models of spirituality. We owe a debt to Roman Catholic theologians, especially liberation theologians, who have taken the lead in questioning a spirituality that was, until very recently, widely accepted and respected among the majority of Christians.

The fact is that the Church does not have appropriate, officially commemorated models or an authentic spirituality suitable for all the baptized.

> The universal call to holiness proclaimed by Jesus and reaffirmed by the Vatican Council has in practice often eluded even the most dedicated spiritual leaders of the Church. We do not have a spirituality of all the baptized, but a presumed state of perfection (the clerical or religious state) which is presented in modified form to everyone else (the laity). . . . With God-given liberty, laity must shed ecclesial management of spirituality and creatively explore a spirituality for all the baptized, not a spirituality derived from clerics and monastics.[7]

NEW PUBLIC MODELS

As long as the laity continue to accept ecclesial management of models and modes of spirituality, their official models for following Jesus will continue to be those the Church says they ought to be. Until the laity liberate themselves from the captivity of clerically determined spirituality, there is nothing to prevent them from identifying models of their own choosing. These models can be both public and personal. Models of public figures might, in time, make it into official calendars of saints; personal models—like one's mother, who lived a sacrificial life, for example— would not be officially recognized. A public model—Martin Luther King, Jr., perhaps—might also be a personal one, but it would be unusual for the converse to be true. Both personal and public models nurture individuals and encourage them on the pilgrim way.

There are four laypersons I would add to the Calendar of Saints as new public models.

I would add Abraham Lincoln (1809–1865), sixteenth president of the United States, a Christian whose faith informed his public role. Lincoln,

like so many others touched by Christ, was a member of no particular
Church. But his life and politics clearly illustrate he did indeed serve Christ
in humanity. It is known that Lincoln was very knowledgeable about the
Bible (he owned several of them) and often quoted from it in private
conversations and public addresses. He began his Gettysburg Address with
the phrase "Four score and seven years ago . . . " rather than by merely
saying, "Eighty-seven years ago."

"Let us judge not, that we be not judged" was quoted in his Second
Inaugural Address. Clearly his faith was manifest in his works. In 1864
a group from Baltimore gave him a Bible. Receiving it, he remarked: "In
regard to this great book, I have to say it is the best gift God has given
to man."[8] Ninety years after his death, a charming, signed devotional book
of daily scriptural readings and prayers—known to have been Lincoln's—
was discovered. It was well worn and had obviously been used often.
It is believed that Lincoln carried the little book with him everywhere.
Why then, inquired Henry C. Deming, congressman from Connecticut,
did Lincoln—a man of obvious faith—not belong to a Church? President
Lincoln replied:

> When any church will inscribe over its altar, as its sole qualification
> for membership, the Savior's condensed statement for the substance
> of both law and Gospel, "Thou shalt love the Lord thy God with
> all thy heart, and with all thy soul, and with all thy mind, and thy
> neighbors as thyself," that church will I join with all my heart and
> soul.[9]

I would add Dorothy Day (1897–1980) of the Catholic Worker movement, who, with Peter Maurin, founded *The Catholic Worker* and spent
all of her adult life serving the poor. Dorothy Day was critical of the
Christianity she observed in the Episcopal Church of her youth. During
her adolescent years she wrote:

> My ideas have changed about Sunday. I have learned that it is rather
> hypocritical to be so strict on Sunday and not on every other day
> of the week. Every day belongs to God and every day we are to
> serve him doing his pleasure. . . . Children look at things very
> directly and simply, I did not see [in church] anyone taking off his
> coat and giving it to the poor. I didn't see anyone having a banquet
> and calling in the lame, the halt and the blind. . . . I wanted life
> and I wanted abundant life. I wanted it for others. . . . I wanted
> everyone to be kind, I wanted every home to be open to the lame,
> the halt and the blind. . . . The ugliness of life in the world which
> professed itself to be Christian appalled me. . . . Where were the
> saints to try to change the social order?[10]

In time Dorothy Day became a Roman Catholic, although she was not unaware of the Church's deficiencies. She became one of those saints who tried to change the social order; she provided homes for the poor, the lame, the halt, the blind, and the destitute.

> We felt a respect for the poor and destitute as those nearest to God, as those chosen by Christ for his compassion. Christ lived among men. The great mystery of the incarnation, which meant that God became man that man might become God, was a joy that made us want to kiss the earth in worship, because his feet had once trod that same earth.[11]

Dorothy Day never wavered in her devotion and service to Christ, and never was she in the slightest doubt as to where he was to be found. The journey to Christ in the other is, as she called it, "The Long Loneliness" (also the title of her autobiography), but it is a long loneliness that leads to abundant life.

Dag Hammarskjöld (1905–1961), of Sweden, international diplomat, peacemaker, and secretary-general of the United Nations, is already among the saints in the Lutheran Calendar. He was a quiet, tactful, and energetic leader in the international community when independence and nationalism in Africa were seeking expression and when France and England were entangled with the Middle Eastern countries in the Suez Canal crisis. Acting as negotiator in these delicate situations, Hammarskjöld proved himself a calm and humane leader. He died in an airplane crash while enroute to the Congo (now Zaire) in Northern Rhodesia (now Zambia).

Hammarskjöld was the son of a former prime minister of Sweden and the grandson of a Lutheran pastor. Like Abraham Lincoln, he was a casual participant in religious services, although he was very devout. As a peacemaker he was among those whom Jesus regarded most highly: "Blessed are the peacemakers, for they shall be called the children of God" (Matt. 5:9). Perhaps he was more reticent about his faith in relationship to his work than we would have wished; nonetheless, his actions demonstrated that he did indeed unite faith and action. In considering this aspect of Hammarskjöld's life, W.H. Auden reflected, "I cannot myself recall another—of an attempt by a professional man of action to unite in one life the *vita activa* and the *vita contemplativa*."[12]

At his death, the notebook that was the record of Hammarskjöld's spiritual journey was found at his bedside. The first entry had been made when Hammarskjöld was twenty years old: "I am being driven forward into an unknown land. The pass grows steeper, the air colder and sharper. A wind from my unknown goal stirs the strings of expectation. . . . Shall

I ever get there"[13] The entire journal, covering thirty-six years, is the account of Hammarskjöld's growth and commitment to the way of the Cross while maintaining an active role as a leader in public life.

He recorded what we might call a "conversion experience," or God's call to him:

> I don't know Who—or What—put the question. I don't know when it was put. I don't even remember answering. But at some moment I did answer *Yes* to Someone—or Something—and from that hour I was certain that existence is meaningful and that, therefore, my life, in self-surrender, had a goal.[14]

Appropriately, he made that entry in his journal on Pentecost, 1961. Its tone is like that of the story of Christ—as the stranger—walking down the Emmaus road and meeting his friends, who did not know his identity: "Two of Jesus' followers were going to a village named Emmaus . . . and they were talking to each other about all the things that had happened. As they talked and discussed, Jesus himself drew near and walked along with them; they saw him but somehow did not recognize him" (Luke 24:13–16). Perhaps Hammarskjöld did not call that "Someone" Christ, but his public actions were surely a response to Christ's call:

> For someone whose job so obviously mirrors man's extraordinary possibilities and responsibilities, there is no excuse if he loses his sense of having been called. So long as he keeps that, *everything* [italics mine] he can do has a meaning, nothing a price.[15]

And Hammarskjöld described a spirituality that nurtured and informed his everyday life:

> God is wholly in you, just as for you, He is wholly in all you meet. With this faith, in prayer you descend into yourself to meet the Other. In the steadfastness and light of this union, [you] see that all things stand, like yourself, alone before God. And that each of your acts is an act of creation, conscious, because you are a human being with human responsibilities, but governed, nonetheless, by the power beyond human consciousness which created man. You are liberated from things, but you encounter in them an experience which has purity and clarity of revelation. In the faith which is God's marriage to the soul, *everything* therefore has a meaning. So live, then, that you may use what has been put into your hand.[16]

Two months before his death, Dag Hammarskjöld recorded this prayer:

In love and in faith,
May we follow Thee,
With self-denial, steadfastness, and courage. . . .
Give us
A pure heart
That we may see Thee,
A humble heart
That we may hear Thee,
A heart to love
That we may serve Thee,
A heart of faith
That we may live Thee.[17]

Jesus never commanded his disciples to think, to contemplate, to consider, to read, to study, to reflect, to ponder; his words were active: feed, heal, go, seek, give, find, sow, plant, build. "As John the Evangelist points out, the only valid and effective love is that which operates in deed and in truth rather than in word and intention."[18] Certainly there is nothing wrong with thinking (unless it inhibits doing), and thoughts always precede action, but Jesus was unmistakably clear about actions: It is actions that feed and heal and plant and sow and work for justice; it is they that extend God's kingdom. God's way, the spiritual way, the way of following Jesus, is in doing. "It is not the person who says 'Lord, Lord,' but the person who *does* the will of my father" (Matt. 7:21–22). The three saints I would add to the calendars, as it happens, have all been persons of words, but it was their actions that invited their inclusion on the list.

Finally, the fourth saint I would add to the list is, like the others, a person of action. He is still living and therefore would not yet qualify for any official Church calendar. (The one characteristic shared by every person on every official calendar of saints is that they have died!) He is mentioned here because his life is representative of the social action that—inspired by the supreme social activist, Jesus Christ—we all aspire to. This living saint is Cesar Estrada Chavez (1927–), an American farm-labor leader of Hispanic descent who, through organizing Mexican and Mexican-American vegetable and fruit pickers, brought about greater justice and improved living and working conditions for the workers. Through strikes, fasts, picketing, demonstrations, and marches, he obtained contracts between workers and growers and, in 1972, was successful in forming the United Farm Workers' Union. When asked how he had approached his enormous task, he replied, "When you pick grapes, you pick a bunch at a time. Eventually you pick a whole vineyard. Organizing is no different."[19]

How, one might wonder, could Chavez's people, exhausted from hard labor in the fields of California under the blistering sun, muster energy enough to meet and organize in the labor camps at night? One way was, simply, by participating in Christ's life through the nurture of the Eucharist. Chavez, a devout Roman Catholic, explained:

> Every day we had a mass, held a meeting, sang spirituals. . . . Those meetings were responsible in large part for keeping the spirit up of our people inside the camp and helping our organizing for the coming battle.[20]

Of course the workers took strength from each other as well. And Chavez did not supervise the unionization from behind a desk; he did not merely write plans of action for others to follow. He showed the people through his own—often costly—actions:

> If we're going to lead people and ask them to starve and really sacrifice, we've got to do it first, do it more than anybody else, because it isn't the orders, it isn't the pronouncements, *it's the deeds that count*.[21]

But what could an impoverished farm leader, leading a struggling band of workers who had almost nothing, use to attain the goals of justice? The workers' only assets were themselves and God working through them:

> We must admit that our lives are all that really belong to us. So it is how we use our lives that determines what kind of men we are. It is my deepest belief that only by giving our lives do we find life.
> I am convinced that the truest act of courage, the strongest act of manliness, is to sacrifice ourselves for others in a totally non-violent struggle for justice.[22]

At times Chavez drew attention through fasting to the injustices endured by farm workers. These facts were often misunderstood, but Chavez tried to explain:

> The fast is a very personal spiritual thing, and it's not done out of recklessness. It's not done out of a desire to destroy myself, but it's done out of a deep conviction that we can communicate to people, either those who are for us or against us, faster and more effectively spiritually than we can any other way.[23]

Whenever Chavez broke a fast, his first food was the bread of the Holy Eucharist, for he acknowledged that he was only able to sustain his work by Christ's word made flesh and dwelling in him.

In addition to all this, Cesar Chavez was sustained by his own heros, in whom God's saving grace was profoundly manifest. "As for us, we have this large crowd of witnesses around us" (Heb. 12:1). Dorothy Day was one such hero. As a frail old lady, an elder stateswoman active in many causes for justice, Dorothy Day joined some of the farm workers' marches and demonstrations. Also there was Senator George McGovern, the Reverend Martin Luther King, Jr., Coretta Scott King, St. Francis, Gandhi, Senator Robert Kennedy, and President John F. Kennedy. The walls of Chavez's tiny bedroom adjoining his office were plastered with pictures of these personal saints. Surely they helped him—and continue to help him—on his journey, just as Cesar Chavez himself, his life and work and witness for justice, encourage us on our way.

Abraham Lincoln, Dorothy Day, Dag Hammarskjöld, Cesar Chavez— these are saints to be admired. They are persons with whom one can identify, whose lives give one strength. But admiration, identification, drawing strength are not enough. If saints are going to be models for the spiritual journey, for the following of Christ, they must become the building blocks of *our* lives of faith and action. They ought not to be merely admired; rather, we are challenged to emulate them, to live lives like theirs. In emulating the saints we are urged to see the world through their eyes, to hear God's people with their ears, to speak with their voices, to walk with their feet, to love with their sensitivity, to build with their hands, to feel with their hearts, to think and know and understand with their minds.

Abraham Lincoln teaches us how to seek justice through government. May we, like him, live lives that promote justice. Like Dorothy Day, may we serve the forgotten people on the fringes of society, for, by serving the poor, Dorothy Day taught us that we serve none other than Christ himself. Like Dag Hammarskjöld, may we in our lives consciously unite the world of faith with the world of action. Emulating him, may we be self-denying, steadfast, and courageous. May our hearts be pure and humble and loving so that we live God in the other. Cesar Chavez responds to the suffering Christ in his people. He aches with their pain and cries their tears. Chavez's life is testimony to what one person, inspired by God's magnificent grace, can do to bring liberation and justice out of oppression. May our own lives be such testimonies.

Following Jesus in the world of government, in the poor, by uniting faith and action, by seeking justice—however difficult—is possible because the saints have shown us the way. They have followed Christ; so may we.

The passionately loving Christ, the persecuted Christ, the lonely Christ, the Christ despairing over God's silence, the Christ who in dying was so totally forsaken, for us and for our sakes, is like the brother or the friend to whom we can confide *everything,* because he knows everything that can happen to us. In our hopes about life, in our activity, in our love of living, we participate in his passion for the kingdom of freedom. Our disappointments, our lonelinesses and our defeats do not separate us from him; they draw us more deeply into communion with him. This is what faith really is, not with head or lips or out of habit, but believing *with one's whole life.* It means seeking community with the human Christ in every situation in life, and in every situation experiencing his own history.[24]

PERSONAL MODELS

Strictly speaking, saints are saints because our Churches tell us they are; churches canonize them, dress them up, give them special days of commemoration, and memorialize them in calendars of saints. These saints are alike in that they have died and are, with few exceptions, well known.

But we know we are also surrounded by a great company of living saints, most of whom no one has ever heard of and who would themselves be astonished to think that someone ever thought of them as saints!

The great cloud of witnesses, loosely speaking, is composed of many of the saints officially recognized by the Churches, public persons like those suggested in the last section of this chapter and those I have termed "personal models." A saint, even an exceptionally well-known one such as St. Francis of Assisi, can only help us learn the spiritual way if in fact he or she helps us follow Jesus. Unless St. Francis really teaches me how I can follow Jesus by following his example and emulating his life, he cannot be a model for my spiritual journey. He must indeed teach me how I can, as he did in his lifetime, become an "instrument of God's peace." Someone else—for example, my grandmother, who was only known and loved by her family and friends—might be a better model for my spiritual journey because she taught me some of what I need to know to try to live my life as a faithful Christian. In learning to follow Jesus it is quite possible my grandmother could teach me a great deal but St. Francis virtually nothing. In that case, my grandmother would be one of my personal models in the spiritual journey, not St. Francis. As it happens, both St. Francis *and* my grandmother, Constance Jackson Shrigley, are on *my* calendar of saints, as are Dag Hammarskjöld, Dorothy Day, Abraham Lincoln, and Cesar Chavez.

Dear reader, you may have noticed that this book was dedicated to about two hundred "lay saints, past and present, ordinary and extraordinary, famous and infamous and obscure; lay saints whose holy living, or being, or music, or courageous political leadership, or writings, or witness, or art have formed the life of the world and, in particular, the life of this writer."[25] All these saints do, in a very direct way, just what the dedication claims—they nurture my life. Many of them have done so during the writing of this book.

While I was thinking through chapter 3, "The Liberation of the Laity," I realized I could not possibly write about spirituality without looking at the lives of those persons I admire who live, or have lived, the spiritual journey. I *write* about following Jesus, but I need the help of those who *live* lives of fidelity to Jesus, models of persons who live Jesus' life and communicate that life through their actions. Through the patterns of their lives they teach me how I, too, can follow Jesus. Just like them.

> The meaning of the imitation of Christ is in itself simple: trying to act in our existential situation in the same way Christ acted in his situation. . . . To imitate Christ does not mean to copy or even imitate his gestures: It means having the same attitude and the same spirit as Jesus, incarnating it in our concrete situation, which is different from that of Jesus.[26]

So the names of the saints began popping into my head: artists, teachers, politicians, family members, neighbors, university professors, garage mechanics, colleagues, baby sitters, sextons, doctors, a lawyer, secretaries, business executives, a university financial-aid officer, bankers, children, a physicians' assistant, a police officer, a filmmaker, a butcher, a so-called heretic, writers, potters, an architect, directors of soup kitchens, directors of shelters for the homeless, and many more. For many years I had been vaguely aware that the memories and examples of special persons in my life were important to me, but only recently has it become clear just how they teach me the lessons I need to know about discipleship.

The names of the people who have shown me the way, who have been my mentors, have helped at crucial times in my life, have shown me how I have fallen short, have illustrated the importance of justice, the meaning of racism, the wonder of laughter, have expanded the narrowness of my vision—these people flooded my mind. I kept a notepad with me and jotted down their names as they arose, each time bringing to mind just why each saint was important to me and what he or she was teaching me. This notebook of saints is becoming a habit. It is with me always.

Every week or so another saint gets added to it. This book is dedicated
to all of them. Those on my list have come to mind in no particular order.
For example, George McGovern, retired senator from South Dakota,
follows David Watts, my garage mechanic. My mother and father's names
are close to those of Mohandas Gandhi and Jacob Epstein, the sculptor.
Most of my personal saints are alive; some have died recently; others lived
in prior ages.

Charles Lawrence was president of the House of Deputies of the
General Convention of the Episcopal Church. Nancy Lambert was a
Dakota Indian from the Rosebud Indian Reservation in South Dakota.
Theodora Glover is a New Haven politican, Louisa Turner is a business
executive, Elisabeth S. Bundy is my mother. Ricardo Pimentel is a guard
at a Jesuit Monastery in the Dominican Republic. Clare Davis is a New
York City film producer, Alice Ruotolo is a baby sitter and housekeeper,
Kevin Leary is a police officer, Hugh Sutherland is a building contractor.
Jorge Lee runs a family Chinese restaurant in Matomoros, Mexico. Harry
Puddyfoot is a butcher in the Woolwich section of London. James DiMeo
was a kindly landlord. Ellen Stanley and Chenda Korm are children. Sally
Palmer and Chris Clark are potters. Ruth Moore runs a soup kitchen in
a storefront. Alene Tate manages a Social Security office. Evelyn Babb
is a maid, Susan Ransom is a parish secretary, Jill Bigwood is a financial-
aid officer. Thomas Hooker is a retired banker. Irene Jackson-Brown is
a church executive, Philip Johnson is an architect, Ransey Cole is a
physician, Courtney Bourns a lawyer.

By emulating the lives of these saints, I am led to a greater participation
in the life and rhythm of God's created order. ''Spirituality . . . is a love
which through faith and hope leads one to a greater share in existence.''[27]
The saints lead me into God's world, to see it from their perspectives
and to feel it with their passions.

David Watts, Raymond Esposito, Nicholas and James Grasso are garage
owners and mechanics. Their work is hard. They pump gasoline outside,
whether it is nine degrees Fahrenheit or ninety-nine, in wind, rain, sleet,
snow, under scorching sun. They do it cheerfully, and in the summer
they give the children Cokes and inner tubes to play with on the beach.
They keep cars, trucks, and vans going. They keep our old car going into
its second hundred thousand miles, and they keep it safe. *Through their
important work they hold together the fabric of everyday life.* They keep
the world moving safely.

Marg VanCleef, Suzanne Abrams, Paul Schattauer, Vincent McGee, and
William Stringfellow are peacemakers. They demonstrate outside nuclear-
submarine plants, they engage in civil disobedience. They picket outside

antiballistic missile sites. They get arrested, they pay for their witness for peace with fines and jail terms. I write about peacemaking; they practice peacemaking. They bother my conscience; they make me feel uneasy, for they put their bodies on the line at the places of sin in society. I know I should also. *Following their example, may I put my body on the line and act for peace in the world.*

A white man who practiced law in Harlem was the first person to teach me the meaning of racism and how middle-class northern liberals were just as racist as anyone else. I heard him lecture when I was a young undergraduate student. He was angry and fiery. His words were true, but he made me nervous and defensive. But he was right, and I needed his hard lesson. This man was William Stringfellow, who wrote about racism in *My People Is the Enemy: An Autobiographical Polemic:*

> First, white people must die to that mentality [of determining how the racial crisis will be resolved] by suffering the hostility and rejection of Negroes and by risking their lives and the future of this society in the hands of the Negroes. This is the preface to reconciliation between black men and white men.[28]

Sometime later, living through the Black Power days of the late 1960s as part of a multiracial student community at the edge of Harlem, I was to learn the painful truth of Stringfellow's words. He helped me understand.

After his death I learned that William Stringfellow had loved the circus and had subscribed to all the circus magazines.[29] I had thought I was the only adult who steals out of the office on a weekday morning to see the circus performers parade from the train station in downtown New Haven to the Coliseum. The next time the circus comes to town I will not feel so silly and childish. Thank you, Bill Stringfellow, for giving me permission to act like a child. Also, Stringfellow prayed for his dogs.[30] Now I will feel less ridiculous when I want to pray for our cat. *May I, like William Stringfellow, have the sensitivity to recognize racism wherever it is found and to fight against it.* May my life, like his, be enriched and lightened by pets and circus parades.

Sidney Trower, Cora Cobey, Suzie Wojewoda, Edith Townsend, and Evelyn Babb are maids and sextons. They keep churches, schools, hotels, and homes clean and orderly. Their work often goes unnoticed because they do it so well. Theirs is the type of work that gets noticed only when it is not done. *May I, like them, take pride in ordinary work that usually goes unnoticed and unappreciated.* Their work contributes to the order and routine of society. *May I also serve the world with care, love, cheerfulness, and patience.*

Ruth Carter, Alice Ruotolo, and Rita Powers are and were baby sitters. In taking care of our children, baby sitters guard and protect our future. Ellen Stanley and Chenda Korm are children. They are life's greatest treasures. Jesus loved children because they are direct, honest, and simple; children responded to him. Children have not settled into defensive and cautious ways; they are not cynical and sarcastic. Baby sitters are like Jesus because they love and protect children. *May we, like baby sitters, protect and guide our children with love, patience, warmth and understanding.*

Several parents of retarded children are models for the spiritual journey. There is also a retarded child on the list. *These saints teach me that each person is loved and adored by God. May I emulate just a bit of that love.*

Although saints are often poor and we are more likely to find Christ among the poor than in the corporate boardrooms, the wealthy can follow Christ, too. It is harder for them to do so, for they have more to lose; they know they must give their riches to the poor. Just like Florence Nightingale. *May we give up our possessions and become poor.*

In this world there will always be great, self-sacrificing spirits who, though belonging to a more favorably placed social group, will join in solidarity with those on the bottom, embody their hopes, and suffer their dire plight.[31]

Jacob Epstein, Sally Palmer, Gretchen Pritchard, Salvador Dali, Chris Clark, Fritz Eichenberg, Jane Hooker, Thomas Daye, and Philip Johnson are sculptors, architects, artists, and potters. Salvador Dali's "Last Supper" depicts the historical event in bold relief. In my teens, I was greatly moved by it. Later I came to prefer Fritz Eichenberg's "Last Supper," in which the disciples are portrayed as street people gathered around a simple kitchen table. Both artists have helped make the Last Supper, and every supper of our Lord, real to me. *May we through the Lord's Supper—the Holy Communion—become that holy community of Christ's body in the world.*

Jacob Epstein, the sculptor who created the magnificent "St. Michael and the Devil" on an outside wall of Coventry Cathedral, said as he prepared to begin the project: "My beliefs can be clearly seen through my work."[32] *May our beliefs, our faith, like that of Jacob Epstein and all the artist-saints, be clearly seen in our work.*

My children—Virginia, Christian, and Perry—and the child who adopted us, John, are on my list of personal saints because they are agents for our transformation. Our children change our lives. Some twenty years ago, as I cradled our first-born, Virginia, I marveled at the perfectly formed, tiny, and delicate package of mystery that had appeared in our lives. Although she was yet just a few minutes old, I became poignantly aware that from that hour on my husband's and my lives would never again be the same. Our children teach us responsibility, they teach us how to love, they teach us that the well-being of other human beings is of far greater importance than our own. Children teach us how to make sacrifices for their sakes, they teach us wonder, imagination, laughter. They teach us the feeling of utter powerlessness: We cannot shield them from disappointments, sorrows, danger. We can suffer with them, but we cannot prevent their suffering. We cannot protect our teenage children from the drunk driver who could—in an instant—cut short their young lives. *Through the wonder of birth we become co-creators with God and participate with God in the care of all creation.*

My mother and father, Elisabeth S. Bundy and Howard Wheeler, are also in my catalog of saints. We appreciate our parents when we ourselves become parents. Our parents literally give us everything with which to begin life. They gave us life itself. Had they done nothing else, that singular gift would have been enough. *Our parents teach us that our life—and every other human life—is God's greatest gift and greatest blessing.*

Old friends are reminders of old journeys; they keep us grounded in the soil of our yesterdays while urging us on into tomorrow. *Our old friends have loved us for most of our lives; they keep us on the track and spur us on into the future.*

With our professional colleagues, our fellow workers at our places of employment, we experience collegiality. Our ideas become better when they are shared with colleagues; our plans become better with our colleagues' help; our colleagues can bring to light that which never occurred to us before. Collegial relationships are important because we spend all our working hours with our fellow workers.

Writers capture life's experiences with words. They articulate our thoughts. Their works give us pleasure, relaxation; they transport us for a while into other realms. Writers tickle our imaginations, they make us laugh, sometimes they change our minds. They tell us the truth about ourselves and society. And some writers teach others how to write— yes, even how to live—and because they have done it, so can I.

The sociologist, critic of American life, and prolific writer C. Wright Mills wrote such sociological classics as *White Collar, The Power Elite,* and *Power, Politics and People.* He is on my list of saints, but not for having written those excellent books; rather, for one twenty-five-page essay entitled "On Intellectual Craftsmanship." Through that essay he taught me that the way persons live their lives and conduct themselves from day to day, their personal experiences, are important not only in the formation of character but in the formation of the professional worker. Mill's writings on the worlds of work, scholarship, everyday living, and experience have taught me how to use *all* experience—personal *and* professional—to inform all my life and work:

> Scholarship is a choice of how to live as well as a choice of a career; whether he knows it or not, the intellectual workman forms his own self as he works towards the perfection of his craft; to realize his own potentialities, and any opportunities that come his way, he constructs a character which has as its core the qualities of a good workman.
>
> What this means is that you must learn to use your life experience in your intellectual work: continually to examine and interpret it. . . . In this sense you are personally involved in every intellectual product upon which you may work. . . . Your past plays into and affects your present and it defines your capacity for future experience.[33]

I do not know whether or not C. Wright Mills was a Christian, but just as Christ plunges us into humanity, Mills teaches me the value of all human experience in the formation of scholars, of human beings. *May I, like C. Wright Mills, value and utilize all human experience.*

Some saints on my calendar are not Christian. How can a non-Christian show me how to become a better Christian? Elie Wiesel shows me that if we forget the massacre of two-thirds of the European Jewish population during the Second World War, we will forget the pervasive power of pure evil and hate and allow the Holocaust to be repeated in our time. May we, like Elie Wiesel, remember inhumanity so that we can protect and honor the humanity of every human being. May we, like Anwar Sadat, work to break down the barriers that divide Moslems, Jews, and Christians. When Mohandas Gandhi was a student in England he became interested in the life of Christ and thought seriously about becoming a Christian. The story is told that he once said he would have become a Christian had he not seen how so many British Christians lived their faith! May we be reminded by Gandhi that, as Christians, we must live the life of Christ that we claim to believe. *The resurrected Christ is with us and active wherever people, regardless of creed, carry forward his cause.*

> Wherever people seek the good, justice, humanitarian love, solidarity, communion, and understanding between people, wherever they dedicate themselves to overcoming their own egoism, making this world more human and fraternal, and opening themselves to the normative Transcendent for their lives, there we can say, with

all certainty, that the resurrected one is present, because the cause for which he lived, suffered, was tried and executed is being carried forward. . . . All who adhere to Jesus' cause are his brothers and sisters and he is acting in them so that there might be greater openness towards others and more human space for God.[34]

There is one saint entered on my list simply as "Joe." I never knew Joe's last name, but I know he was like Christ. In every way he was a servant of others, just like Christ.

Joe was very frail and worn-looking. He was probably years younger than his stooped appearance suggested. Although he wasn't particularly articulate, he had a certain indefinable presence about him. In the housing development where I live, Joe did the jobs no one else wanted to do. On bitterly cold days, when anyone with any sense would have been inside in front of a warm fire, Joe would be out plowing the sidewalks and driveways for the three hundred or so residents. On such days he could be seen wearing his Army surplus jacket, hunkered down against the blustering winds, visibly struggling to push back the rapidly accumulating snow. In summer he pushed an inefficient-looking lawnmower around the grounds, often under the blistering midday sun. Tiredness must have been his constant state, but I never heard so much as a whisper of complaint pass his lips.

Nights before trash days Joe would check the bins and dumpsters for discarded furniture, junk others might consider treasures. He gave some of these "gifts" away in the neighborhood; the rest he took into town for distribution among the poor. He gave me flowers in the spring and advice on home repairs the year round. When I needed a little paint for a touch-up, he got it. I don't think Joe ever made much money, and my guess is he probably was not treated very well by the development's management.

When the landlord died, Joe and I went to the funeral and sat together. When we went up to receive the communion, it was refused him. The memory of the priest's words to Joe that late September morning still sears me: "You're not a Catholic." Perhaps not, but he was better than a Catholic; Joe was a saint.

I do not know what happened to Joe; things changed after the landlord's death. But what I do know is this: *Joe's life and example epitomizes for me the true meaning of Christ. Joe's life gives life—flesh and blood—to my understanding of Christ as the person for others, the loving servant of all.* Perhaps it is the likes of Joe whom the hymn writer had in mind when he wrote about the stars appearing before God's throne:

Who are these like stars appearing,
These before God's throne who stand?
Each a golden crown is wearing;
Who are all this glorious band? . . .

These are they whose hearts were riven,
    Sore with woe and anguish tried,
Who in prayer full oft have striven
    With the God they glorified. . . .

These, like priests, have watched and waited,
    Off'ring up to Christ their will,
Soul and body consecrated,
    Day and night they serve him still.
        Now in God's most holy place,
        Blest they stand before his face.[35]

Saint Joe is on my list because his life is an elegant example of Christian living at its best. He is there also to represent all those other saints whose names I know not but to whom I am, nonetheless, indebted, those whose kindnesses, little and big, have added to my life: the truck driver who retrieved the duffel bag that had blown off my car roof on a Pennsylvania highway and who took considerable pains to get it back to me; the lifeguard who rescued my son, Chris, from the murky bottom of a small-town swimming pool; the Italian grandmother who took me into her home and gave me a steaming hot plate of pasta that cold and rainy day when I was doing a neighborhood survey on her street; all the strangers and fellow travelers in foreign lands who have helped me along the way and who have, in innumerable ways, shown me the way of Christ. Joe represents them. *Like the Unknown Soldier entombed in Washington, who represents all soldiers of all wars who have given their lives for their country, Joe represents all the unknown persons to whom I owe my life.*

Finally, there are the lessons taught us by the dying, those stars who are about to appear in God's most holy place. It is paradoxical that the dying saints, hovering on the threshold of eternity, often plunge us more completely into this temporal realm. How often in the presence of the dying do we appreciate the wisdom they bring to our lives. How often does the dying person's weak hand in ours impart strength to our whole body and give us courage to continue as Christ's strong body in the world. And the dying teach us, by their example, to die gracefully and peacefully and that God will indeed give us that grace and peace when the time will come. They teach us that nothing can separate us from God's love and that therefore we need only let go and embrace eternity. The meaning of death is defined by the meaning of life, and the meaning of life by the meaning of death. Following the saints, surrounded by the magnificent company of that great cloud of witnesses, *may we faithfully follow Christ in our living and in our dying.*

This long excursus into my own personal calendar of saints and how its members teach me to follow Jesus is intended to be more than my way of honoring my heroes. Rather, its point is to suggest that we all can have models for the spiritual journey, models of persons past and present, living and dead, ordinary and extraordinary, famous and infamous and obscure; lay and ordained saints whose holy living, or dying, or being, or music, or courageous political leadership, or writings, or witness, or art have formed the life of the world and the Church as well as our own lives. These models are often right here with us, some of them living in our memories. Saints can be found among family members, friends, colleagues, in our churches, in the neighborhoods where we live. They are store clerks and mechanics, lawyers, police, business executives, maids and janitors; they are in every place, in every community. To identify them, we need only peer into the recesses of our memories and look around us. They are with us everywhere. They are memorialized in the Churches' calendars of saints; their names are engraved on our hearts and in our memories. Whether living or dead, they run life's races with us; they are our models for following Jesus. Our companions along the route, they are our cheering section. To join them, to run with them, we need only sensitize ourselves to their presence. "Since we are surrounded by so great a cloud of witnesses . . . let us run with perseverance the race that is set before us" (Hebrews 12:1–2).

CHAPTER 8

KEEPING STABLE THE FABRIC
OF THE WORLD

> Lay people are not to flee from temporal realities in
> order to seek God. They are to remain present and
> active amid those realities, and there find the Lord.
> —*Puebla Document*

FOLLOWING JESUS IN EVERYDAY LIFE

How can he become wise who handles the plow . . . who drives
oxen and is occupied with their work, and whose talk is about bulls?
He sets his heart on plowing furrows, and he is careful about fodder
for this heifers. So too is every craftsman and master workman who
labors by night as well as by day; those who cut the signets of seals,
each is diligent in making a great variety; he sets his heart on
painting a lifelike image, and he is careful to finish his work. So
too is the smith sitting by the anvil, intent upon his handiwork in
iron; the breath of the fire melts his flesh, and he wastes away in
the heat of the furnace; he inclines his ear to the sound of the
hammer, and his eyes are on the pattern of the object. He sets his
heart on finishing his handiwork, and he is careful to complete its
decoration. So too is the potter sitting at his work and turning
the wheel with his feet; he is always deeply concerned over his
work. . . . He moulds the clay with his arm and makes it pliable
with his feet; he sets his heart to finish the glazing, and he is careful
to clean the furnace. All these rely upon their hands, and each is
skillful in his own work. Without them a city cannot be established,
and men can neither sojourn nor live there. . . . They keep stable
the fabric of the world, and their prayer is in the practice of their
trade (Ecclus. 38:25–32, 34, RSV).

Laypeople employed in the occupations of the world "keep stable the
fabric of the world, and their prayer is in the practice of their trade."
An essential step in the recovery of an appropriate spirituality for all
persons is to look around and recognize in each other and in every aspect

of human activity the ways in which Jesus is manifested, made known, and followed. Models of persons whom we identify as followers of Jesus—these saints can help us. As we focus on their holy lives, as we emulate them, we are invited to recognize in our own lives the ways we, too, are following Jesus and the ways we can follow him more nearly.

A *recovery* of a spirituality appropriate for all persons is needed rather than the *development* of such a spirituality. "Development" suggests we are building something from scratch, something brand new, whereas in recovering we are bringing back something that once was. The author of Ecclesiasticus suggests a centuries-old spirituality, one we might dust off and put into use in our own day. It is a spirituality that recognizes and assigns worth to maintaining the fabric—the rhythm and structure—of the world; it recognizes being and behaving and prayer that *is* action, prayer that *is* the practice of occupation.

The Churches have not helped people appreciate the formative value of everyday experience, nor how we follow Christ through the everyday activities of our lives. Unless one is a doctor or a nurse, or a teacher, or perhaps a social worker, or is employed in any of the many jobs that directly serve people, one does not generally see how a person follows Jesus through employment. Of course most people have a sense that any job ought to be done well and possibly with a certain sense of pride, but rarely do we attribute religious meaning to ordinary work, nor do we attempt to determine the ways Jesus is, or could be, followed through the ordinary tasks of the world. What about the steel worker, the supermarket clerk, the mechanic, the bus driver, the road contractor, the computer programmer, the secretary, the butcher, the baker, the railway worker, the waitress, the plumber, the printer? How is Jesus served in these occupations? According to the author of Ecclesiasticus, the driver of oxen, the craftsman, the master workman, the smith, the potter "keep stable the fabric of the world," and furthermore, "their prayer *is* in the practice of their trade."

That we have lost a sense of the dignity of human labor and its essential contribution to the very structure of this world has had a devastating effect on the world and the Church. Wherever dignity and appreciation for common tasks are absent, the fabric of society is threatened. All about us we see evidence of poor workmanship and neglect of our physical environment. And because the Church has long since lost any sense of a theology of work or a spirituality of the marketplace, it has lost touch with both the workaday world and the workers. Consequently, workers have grasped neither the meaning of their work nor its profound importance to the maintenance of the fabric of the temporal world, nor have they understood that it is through their work that Christ is recognized and served.

The relationship between persons and their work has always been complex, as has the meaning and significance of work. Prayer has been, at times, intimately related to work. In some ages work—as an instrument of self-purification, discipline, or repentence, or as an expression of charity—has been endowed with religious significance. Manual labor, especially, was given an important place in monastic tradition. But in other ages the monks, Benedictines in particular, have parceled out their manual work to serfs, lay brothers, and lay employees so as to be able to give primacy to prayer and meditation. Meditation has been seen both as a part of daily work and as apart from daily work.

Work has been considered not only necessary but "good." American Protestants raised the understanding of work to a fine art, even an ethic. Often it is said that the Protestant "work ethic" made America great, forgetting the exploitation of minorities that shored up the work ethic and made it work. Historically there have been certain people and classes who have never worked. The world has always known a leisure class—nobles, aristocrats, playboys—who have never needed or wanted to work.

There has always been another leisure class, those with enforced or involuntary leisure, the unemployed: the young, the elderly, the disabled, the ill, and others who for a variety of reasons have been unable to get or keep jobs. Strictly speaking, however, these people are not "leisured" because leisure, in its classic sense, is neither enforced nor involuntary.

Work imparts status. It determines lifestyle and social standing and contributes to self-understanding. Whether one is an employee, an employer, or self-employed may be crucial in determining one's self-image and outlook on life. Do I work for myself? Do I work for someone else? The world looks different from the perspective of a prominent divorce lawyer than it does from that of the local pharmacist or shipping clerk. Then there are issues of power related to work: Do I exercise power in my job, or am I subject to someone else's power?

Whether we like it or not, we are identified with our work and, depending on what the job is and how we feel about it, we may be pleased or displeased to be so identified. If one were to ask the question "Who are you?" the answer would almost certainly be given in terms of the job you do.

Some governments have defined work as a right, like life and liberty. Work can build up, enhance, beautify, glorify. It can also exploit, oppress, and violate. Because work is regarded as not only necessary but desirable

and good, what about the unemployed? Because work is "good," un-
employment must be "bad" and idleness worst of all. If work confers
status, does that mean the unemployed have none?

What about the fruits of labor, the products and the conditions under
which they are produced? Does it matter whether the worker makes
bombs or bicycles, textbooks or toxic chemicals, mattresses or missiles?
Are some jobs more morally or ethically acceptable than others in terms
of what they produce? Are there some industries whose products are
morally unquestionable but which engage in labor practices that oppress
or exploit? Are there some businesses or industries in which Christians
of good conscience ought not to work? Could a Christian work in the
agricultural-products division of a chemical company rather than the
division that produces chemical weapons? Or should the Christian not
work for *any* of that company's divisions? What can be said of the
responsibilities of Christians who are shareholders and board members
of companies whose products are morally questionable? And what about
personal need or necessity: What if the only plant in the area that is hiring
happens to be an armaments factory? Where no other employment is
available, what should the Christian worker do?

With these pressing questions, conflicts of values, and ambiguities
surrounding work, why is it that the Churches have not made it their
business to confront them? The Church pays ample lip service to the
world, work, and the environment, but for all practical purposes it has
lost touch with the issues. They are crying to be addressed.

A MINER'S MINISTRY

The following story, which George Peck, a Baptist theologian, tells about
his father, is all too familiar:

> My father was a coal miner in Australia. He worked in that
> industry for nearly 40 years. During the whole time he was also
> a devout Christian and for most of the time he was a deacon in
> our local Baptist church. There is no doubt that he brought to bear
> upon his life in the mines the Christian faith which he professed.
> He did not hesitate to testify to Christ, and in all kinds of ways
> his commitment to the Gospel in day to day situations, in special
> circumstances (such as through his role in the Mines Rescue Brigade),
> and in the industry itself throughout the district in which he lived.
> But my father always had within him a secret disappointment. He
> wanted to be a minister. He certainly was a preacher (for at least
> three different denominations), and a Sunday School teacher. He

was a leader in his local congregation at several important points. He helped raise a Christian family (his two sons were ordained and his only daughter became a missionary). But as far as he was aware, and as far as his church led him to believe, he was never able to fulfill the one desire which had often been uppermost in his mind. Lacking the education and the opportunity, he had never been able to become a minister.

Not long ago, I would not have thought there was anything strange about my father's experience. I would have taken it for granted that he was right in the conclusion about his life. God had not called him to the ministry . . . he remained a coal miner, and as such, just an "ordinary" Christian.

[But recent experience has made me] seriously dissatisfied with this evaluation of who and what my father was. He lived as a Christian where God had placed him. He made a significant impact on his environment as a servant of Christ. On many occasions he took stands and pursued courses of action because he was convinced they were required of him as a Christian. He ministered, if anyone did, to individuals, to the structures of his society, to his community. . . . The neighborhood, the organizations, the mines of our region were better because Ted Peck lived and worked there and was not afraid to minister the Gospel.

Yet neither he nor his church ever thought of him as a minister or of his service as ministry. He was not acknowledged in that way. . . .[1]

Ted Peck was a leader in his local congregation and a preacher in others. He was a caring and humane worker among his fellow miners. He took stands when his faith required him to do so. The evidence indicates he did indeed follow Christ, both in and out of Church. He did not regard himself as a minister. He did not appreciate the importance of his Christian bearing in the mines, nor, it appears, did his Church help him recognize his ministry. Because of this neglect, Ted Peck "always had within him a secret disappointment."[2] How tragic, how unnecessary, and how familiar is the story!

Throughout its long history, the Church's temptation has been to reduce God's goal of universal salvation to the narrow (and mistaken) understanding of the Church as the exclusive place and vehicle of salvation. Such a minimalist view of the scope of God's reign has led to false dichotomies between the world and the Church, the sacred and the secular, the life of the flesh—flesh often being interpreted as sinful—and the life of the spirit. God only knows how many hundreds and thousands of Ted Pecks there have been who have felt themselves failures only because they were not caught up in the Church's officially ordained ministries. Almost sixty years ago the British missionary Roland Allen, whose forward-looking ideas on ministry went virtually unnoticed in his time, insisted there can be no division between sacred and secular if by secular one means nonreligious:

> We cannot divide life into two compartments, one secular and the other religious. We often talk like that; put in practice it is impossible, and the principle is false. Such a division is utterly opposed to the teaching of the New Testament. For Christian men all work is Christ's, not part of it; He claims the whole of it.
>
> There can be no such thing as secular business for a Christian man. . . . In our Baptismal Service we are told that "Baptism doth represent unto us our profession, which is to follow our Saviour Christ and to be made like unto him." That is a purely spiritual conception of profession. It does not depend at all upon the means of livelihood of the baptized. He [or she] may be a tinker, or tailor, or physician, or lawyer. Whatever his means of livelihood may be, he is bound by that profession. He can follow his Saviour Christ in any walk of life and be made like unto Him. His profession covers all types of work and includes all the acts of life. The whole life is bound up and unified in it.[3]

OUT OF DARKNESS INTO GOD'S MARVELLOUS LIGHT

Twenty years ago, in a Protestant response to Vatican II's positions on the Christian laity, Cynthia Wedel said:

> In considering the challenges facing the Christian Church in the fast-moving, urban, technological world of today, there is ground for the thesis that *nothing is more urgent* for the renewal of the Church than a radical look at the apostolate of the laity. This is equally true of all churches—Protestant, Orthodox and Catholic.[4]

Mrs. Wedel's words have gone mostly unheeded, and, as yet, no denomination has addressed the serious, profound, and far-reaching issues of work and worklessness. Several Churches, however, have recently cited the need for a spirituality appropriate to laypersons who are attempting to live lives of fidelity to Christ where they are, without fleeing the temporal world.

The *Puebla Document* on the mission of the Church in Latin America clearly states the case for an everyday spirituality (its recommendations are equally appropriate to the North American Church):

Through the witness of their lives, timely speaking out, and concrete action, the laity have the responsibility of giving order to
temporal realities and placing them in the service of the task of
establishing God's Kingdom. . . . Lay people should contribute to
the Church as a whole their own experience of sharing in the
problems, challenges, and urgent needs of their "secular world"—
their world of persons, families, social groups, and peoples. . . .
The laity, by virtue of their life experiences, their scholarly, professional, and work competence, and their Christian understanding,
can make a precious contribution by offering all they can to
examining, investigating, and developing the social teaching of the
Church.

    An important aspect of this formation has to do with delving
deeper into a spirituality that is more suited to the status of the
lay person. Some of the essential dimensions of such a spirituality
are the following:

—Lay people are not to flee from temporal realities in order to seek
    God. They are to remain present and active amid those realities,
    and there find the Lord.
—To this presence and activity they are to add the inspiration of
    faith and a sense of Christian charity.
—Through the light of faith, they are to discover the presence of
    the Lord in that reality . . .[5]

"God's People in Ministry," a report on the laity to the Lutheran
Church in America, affirmed the following:

As a people of God we affirm our *vocation*. Our vocation is God's
call to us to use our roles and positions of responsibility to live
out the love we have in Jesus Christ. We are called to be followers
of Jesus Christ both in who we are and what we do: our decisions,
our relationships with others, our work for justice and peace within
our communities and the structures of society, our care of the
environment, our being part of global networks. In all of life's
arenas, we are sustained and strengthened by the knowledge that
we are called out of darkness into God's marvellous light. In
response, we are empowered by the Holy Spirit and sent to express
our faith in Christ within the joys and sufferings of the ordinary
world. We are called to live in love for our neighbor, not counting
the cost. Our vocation is to give ourselves in ministry for the life
of the world . . .

    As people called by God, we affirm that we are *Christ's living
body in the world*. Only by serving God in the world, individually
and corporately, is the Church faithful to Jesus Christ. The whole
body, of which we are a part, serves Christ in ministering wherever

it goes. We recognize that the entire Body, doing what Christ the head directs, is needed to proclaim, teach, show, and do the will of God. We bring to the world the resources of the Christian community. In the suffering and joys of our daily ministry we die and rise with Christ.[6]

What is required for the Church to be fully present and fully at service in the everyday world is nothing less than a radical shift from Church to world and from clerical to lay, and nothing more than a conversion—yes, conversion—to lay responsibility. No more ought we to hear about a "clericalized laity," the very phrase, and most especially the ethos that has given it meaning, needs to be eradicated from our vocabulary. The *Puebla Document* is quite specific on the issue of keeping the laity authentically lay: "They are not to be clericalized . . . for that would overlook the fundamental mission of lay people, which is their involvement in temporal realities. . . ."[7] No more clericalization in any form; rather, it is time for all Christians seriously to consider the implications and the benefits of a "layized" clergy: a body of clergy who would be genuinely inspired and shaped by the experiences of laypersons living out their ministries in the world; whose teaching, pastoral, and sacramental ministries would be thoroughly informed by the work of the Church's primary ministers, the laity; and who would structure their parishes to affirm and support such lay ministries. Why does such a simple truth have to be emphasized again and again as if it were some *avant-garde* pronouncement rather than biblical truth, that Christ came for the world, Christ lived and died for the world, Christ rose again for the world? Not the Church. That biblical truth, that fact, ought to be all that is required, always and everywhere, to keep the focus of *every* ministry on and in the world, extending God's kingdom through the people who follow Christ in the world. Nothing is more crucial, nothing more necessary and pressing than the calling of the Church back to its primary responsibility, that of being Christ's servant and prophetic community in the world.

For the necessary shift to occur, the laity must wake from their slumber. Perhaps the ordained of the Church will help, but the laity are the primary ministers of the Church, and they, therefore, must take the primary responsibility for its transformation. Laypersons must look around them and recognize the ways they are already serving Jesus in society. They must elaborate and extend their ministries of the marketplace. If they do not know whether or not they are serving Christ where they are working, if they question the ethics of their work (or the lack of them), they must seek help in finding answers and making any required changes. Much ministry does indeed occur unconsciously, as the example of Ted Peck illustrates, but such ministries ought to be made conscious and be extended. The transformation will be aided by the recovery of a spirituality—a way of following Jesus—that takes root in everyday life and finds expression in every community.

A SPIRITUALITY OF THE FABRIC

The Christian life must, as Bonhoeffer insisted, be a worldly life. Yet it must be a life of "holy worldliness," of "sacred secularity". . . . Expect to meet God in the way, not to turn aside from the way.[8]

An appropriate spirituality, a way to meet [and to follow] God in the way," is what I have called a "spirituality of the fabric," for laypersons in their daily lives and work "keep stable the fabric of the world, and their prayer is the practice of their trade" (Ecclus. 38:34). It is in keeping stable the fabric of the world that they must expect to find the meaning of existence, the keys to a just society, the love of their lives, the fulfillment of humanity's hopes, the power of their prayer.

A spirituality of the fabric will find expression in occupations that actively serve God's people, among, for example, police and firefighters, hospital workers, teachers. The ministries of these persons, and of those in similar positions, are fairly obvious.

A spirituality of the fabric will find expression in occupations that keep the structures of society intact and operating smoothly. I have a friend who repairs the engines of the town's heavy road machinery; he fixes trucks of all kinds. As soon as snow is predicted, he attaches plows to the vehicles and readies the motors. Much of his work is done in the still hours of the morning, while most of the townspeople sleep. When the snowfall is severe and skilled drivers are needed, Charlie plows the streets. Were it not that Charlie and I are members of the same congregation I would not be aware of his work and would probably take clear, clean streets in a snowy winter for granted. Charlie certainly keeps stable the fabric of society in his necessary work, work that keeps social structures intact.

An important aspect of lay spirituality is recognition. Charlie, by keeping, repairing, and operating the town's road machinery, does *necessary* work. But does he see his work as ministry? Does he see it as a way of following Christ? My guess is that Charlie neither recognizes nor appreciates his important service. A spirituality of the fabric would bring us to appreciate those necessary but largely invisible tasks essential to the smooth running of public life, and to value the important contributions workers make to creation.

Many people have jobs that yield essential products, those necessary to life and health: farm workers, fishermen, ranchers, pharmaceutical manufacturers, bakers and all manner of food production workers (canners, pickers, meat-processing plant workers). They are God's co-creators and coworkers because they supply humankind's basic needs.

It may be difficult to see how some jobs contribute to the fabric of society—the multitude of office and factory jobs, for example—until one looks closely at what they produce. One might wonder how Christ is served through the manufacture of steel products. But if the steel factory produces the girders needed so that bridges in the interstate highway system can be spanned with sturdy and strong materials, then the ministry of steel production can be more easily understood. The same is true of assembly-line workers in automobile plants. Almost everyone has at least one car. Strong, safe, well-manufactured cars are essential to life and safety.

In the most basic way, people follow Jesus through their being—their attitudes, thoughts, ideas, feelings, bearing, and behaving. Spirituality encompasses being. Perhaps the job is tedious and routine. It is probably safe to say that most work is unsatisfying, unrewarding, unexciting, boring. Untold numbers of people simply tolerate their jobs—no more than that—and are kept going by necessity and the promise of weekly pay. But however routine most work may be, human relationships on any job are never routine. Whatever our jobs, we commonly spend many hours of every day with our fellow workers, hours that add up to weeks, months, years. Our fellow employees have babies, family weddings, and funerals, get divorced. Their children get arrested for drunk driving; they graduate from college. Their children get married and have children. They get thrown out of apartments; they buy houses. They participate in parent-teacher associations; they attempt to influence local boards of education; they coach Little League baseball. They watch situation comedies and Monday night football; they win and lose in the state lottery. Our fellow workers represent every stage of life, every age, every human activity, every passion, all of life's joys and failings; they are part of every aspect of God's creation. The respect, consideration, care, even sympathy with which we approach our fellow workers is important, just as we are appreciative of the respect and sympathy shown us. By our being, through our being, we serve Christ in our fellow workers, just as we, too, are served. Being is a ministry of presence, being there, being present. Its importance to the fabric of the world cannot be overestimated, because wherever Christians are, so also is Christ.

Being and the ministry of presence are necessary because of the many unemployed persons who nonetheless seek and serve Christ wherever they are. If Christians were content to be Christian rather than to be identified with their jobs (or lack of them), a whole spirituality of being and presence would naturally evolve. Needed is a spirituality that answers "I am a Christian above all else" to the question "Who are you?" A spirituality of being and presence.

There are some jobs in which Christians—or anyone, for that matter—should not be engaged, because they are inconsistent with Jesus' teachings or do not contribute to the welfare of God's creation, either by *what* they produce or the *way* they are produced. Anything that would harm or destroy physical creation or creatures is suspect—certain chemicals or machinery, for instance, or pornography or anything else that degrades persons. It is difficult and risky to assert but assert it we must: Christians should neither work in industries producing questionable products nor serve on such companies' executive boards (unless by doing so they can effect healthy change).

Some industries and businesses' products are not questionable, but the production *workers* are exploited. Christians ought not to tolerate exploitation or injustice of any kind in any employment setting.

A spirituality of the fabric will find expression in occupations that actively serve God's people and keep intact the social and physical structures of the world. A necessary aspect of such a spirituality will be the recognition of hitherto unrecognized ministries. It will elaborate and extend such ministries. Some work yields products that supply human-kind's basic needs. Workers in these fields are God's co-creators and coworkers. Christians follow Christ through their being and presence. By being, behaving, and believing, Christ is served and honored in fellow workers. Being is of major importance in the recovery of a spirituality of the fabric because it does not need to be rooted in a particular job to find expression; rather, it is lived wherever human beings live and move and have their being. As Oscar Romero has said:

> Let each one of you, in your own job, in your vocation—nun, married person, bishop, priest, high school or university student, workman, laborer, market woman—each one in your own place live the faith intensely and feel that in your surroundings you are a true microphone of God our Lord.[9]

In evolving a realistic spirituality appropriate to the people of his region, Gustavo Gutiérrez said, "We drink from our own wells."[10] And so must we. Drinking out of our own wells, we will drink of living water. By taking nurture from our own soil, our own roots will be grafted to the true vine, the vine that is none other than Christ. Soil, wells, and roots are the fabric of the world; they are the wellsprings of our prayer and our spirituality. In them Christ is sought and found, followed and adored.

> In that world, both created and redeemed by God's love, we expect to find signs of God's loving presence. We expect at all times and in all places to meet God who precedes his Church. God's love does not therefore call us out of the world but rather it constrains us to keep his commandments in the world. In following along the way Christ leads us, we will know joy even as we are asked to allow the world's pain and suffering to touch us as it touched our Lord.[11]

CHAPTER 9

WHERE JESUS WANTS
TO BE FOLLOWED

We must seek Jesus among the undernourished
children who have gone to bed tonight without eating,
among the poor newsboys who will sleep covered with
newspapers in doorways.

—Oscar Romero,
Christmas Eve, 1979,
The Church Is All of You

CHRIST THE MODEL

The mind of God was laid bare in the historical event of Jesus. Through
Jesus has the true and cosmic nature of God been revealed; through him
have the purest possibilities for persons been realized. For insight into
both the nature of God and the extent of human potential, Christ is the
supreme model. He is the two-way window through which the meaning
of God and the meaning of humanity are made known. This is the meaning
of Jesus: perfect God, perfect person. To learn the riches of God, look
to Jesus; to know the best and most altruistic of humankind, look to Jesus.

To discover what Christ the man was like, one need only look to the
people he liked, those with whom he surrounded himself, those he served
and affirmed and defended and loved. Following Jesus, we too ought to
be led into the same kind of company he kept, for as Boff has said so
eloquently:

Fundamentally a Christian has opted to imitate and follow Christ.
. . . The meaning of the imitation of Christ is in itself simple: trying
to act in our existential situation in the same way Christ acted in
his situation. . . . To imitate Christ means having the same attitude
and the same spirit as Jesus, incarnating it in our concrete situation.[1]

Where does God want to be met, encountered, imitated, sought, found,
and followed? In a phrase: God wants to be known and made known
in the poor.

In Luke 6:20–23 and Matthew 5:3–12 Jesus addressed his disciples (and
us) by reminding them that happiness and blessings are to be found among

the poor, those who mourn, the humble, the hungry, the persecuted, the peacemakers, the excluded, those relegated to the margins of society. They are members of God's kingdom, they see God, they receive God's comfort, they will be satisfied, they will receive mercy. Indeed, God calls them his children. Furthermore, it is in the hungry and the thirsty, in the stranger, in the naked (i.e., those who have nothing), in the sick and the imprisoned that Christ is to be found (Matt. 25:31–46).

Of course Jesus is to be followed in the lives of canonized saints, through our daily lives and work, in our friends, neighbors, and colleagues, in our personal models, in the causes to which we are committed, through the liturgy. Jesus is to be followed and adored in all the ways I have described in the previous three chapters. But the *best* way to follow Jesus is to imitate his life in our lives, by living with and serving those in our day who are like the people with whom he lived and whom he served in his. The difference is like experiencing the refreshing space of a city park and then the vast expanse of a sweeping Montana landscape. Space can be encountered anywhere, everywhere, but it is best encountered in some places rather than in others. Thus it is with entering into the life and ministry of Jesus. Jesus is best met in those to whom he gave special attention, in those persons on the periphery—the poor, the captive, the oppressed.

Unfortunately the Church in most parts of the developed world has been largely deaf to this message. Christians wonder why they have difficulty feeling the excitement of faith, the vitality of Jesus, the joy of believing. They mortify the flesh, withdraw into retreats, seek answers from monastics and mystics. They implore priests to give them plans for the development of the spiritual life, ministers to draw the map to God. But how often do we drive by the street person or the shopping-bag lady on our way to a prayer meeting, or pass by the unemployed drinking beer on the front steps of derelict apartment buildings while we rush to the diocesan commission meeting? Or do we take another route altogether, to avoid that part of the city where society's ills are most manifest?

We have difficulty finding and following Jesus because we look in the wrong places. We will do everything and anything, it seems, often at great cost to ourselves and our checkbooks, to follow Jesus—everything, that is, except what Jesus said. And then we will cloister ourselves away in our homes and neighborhoods, behind our sophisticated electronic burglar-alarm systems, confident that the Neighborhood Watch and our deadbolt locks will keep the poor at bay for yet another day. Seventy years ago Charles Gore wrote:

The modern church has generally been on the wrong side. Can we deny it? Can we deny that its conceptions of property and of the obligations of property, and its attitude towards the real needs of the masses of men who have not held property, or have no adequate supply of what life needs for its development, have been wholly different from what the teaching of the prophets and our Lord, and our Fathers in Christendom would have had them to be? In this respect, as in others, our religion is on trial. The place it is to hold in the minds of men in general and in the genuineness which can be ascribed to our profession of brotherhood, depend on our courageous readiness to think again what our Christian principles mean. What do we honestly believe is God's will for men? What do we mean when we say that we hold our property as stewards for God's purposes? Do we really acknowledge that if we are failing to redeem our brothers and sisters from misery and want, we are failing to redeem Christ? And if we genuinely mean what we should mean, and believe what we say, are we, as Christians, ready for a deep and courageous and corporate act of penance and reparation?[2]

Poverty is a persistent theme of both the Old and New Testaments. In them the poor are portrayed as beggars, as those who lack the means to satisfy even their existential needs. They labor under a great weight; bent over, crushed, they lack strength and vigor, they are humiliated.[3]

The Medellin Document classifies the biblical themes of poverty in three categories:

Poverty, as a lack of the goods of this world necessary to live worthily as men, is in itself evil. The Prophets denounce it as contrary to the will of the Lord and most of the time as the fruit of the injustice and sin of men.

Spiritual poverty is the theme of the poor of Yahweh (Zeph. 2:3; Luke 1:46–55). Spiritual poverty is the attitude of opening up to God, the ready disposition of one who hopes for everything from the Lord (Matt. 5:3). Although he values the goods of this world, he does not become attached to them and he recognizes the higher value of the riches of the Kingdom (Amos 2:6–7, 4:1; Jer. 5:28; Mic. 6:12–13; Isa. 10:2 *passim*).

Poverty of commitment, through which one assumes voluntarily and lovingly the conditions of the needy of this world in order to bear witness to the evil which it represents and to spiritual liberty in the face of material goods, follows the example of Christ who took to himself all the consequences of men's sinful condition (Phil. 2:5–8) and who "being rich became poor" (2 Cor. 8:9) in order to redeem us.[4]

It is painful to study the maps in David Barrett's *Encyclopedia of World Religions* of international Church growth, for they reveal, in stark, bold color, little or no growth in the numbers of Christians in the United States and in most of Northern Europe. In fact, in some European countries the number of Christian adherents is declining. By contrast, the maps show explosive growth in most of Central America, parts of South America, and throughout Africa (except in the Moslem world, of course).[5] Organized Christianity is actually growing in some of the nations in which religious liberty is restricted.[6] Ironically, Church growth is either very slow or declining in those areas of the world where there is the most religious broadcasting—Christian radio and television stations—in the U.S.A. and most of Western Europe.[7] What is to be inferred from Barrett's maps? Very rapid growth in several areas of the world, little or no growth in other regions, notably the developed world. Why is there so marked a difference?

The single characteristic shared by the Churches of Central and South America and those of Africa, the common factor transcending ethnic groups and denominations, is that they are poor. By and large, these are communities of the poor. Poor Churches. Naturally the reasons for Church growth, or the lack of it, are varied and complex; nonetheless, I am convinced that poverty can be singled out as being intimately related to the appeal and phenomenal growth of Christianity in poor countries. Furthermore I would contend that the poor of First World nations have not left the Church but that the Church has left them by forgetting poverty's centrality to the meaning and practice of Christianity and by short-changing the Gospel message, robbing it of its power to heal and transform the life of the world.

WHY THE POOR?

Let us consider what is so special about the poor, that which compels us to follow Jesus among them.

The poor are like Jesus. Jesus the man had nothing material save the clothes on his back, and ultimately even those were taken from him. He had no home; he had left the family of his birth; he had no children in the traditional sense; he did not eat regular meals. He was often misunderstood by even his closest friends. For example, they were often bewildered when, unannounced, he would slip away to pray. And although he was loved by his immediate associates, he was despised by the civil and religious authorities. Jesus was a person stripped of everything, even his life, his physical existence. Just like the poor. The poor, being stripped of everything material, are also stripped of pretense, assumptions, pride, selfishness, arrogance. The poor are humble, for the world has humiliated them. They know oppression, for they have been oppressed. They know justice because they have been denied it. They know hate because they have been hated. They are not strangers to failure because, by society's standards, they have failed. They know how it is to be passed over, ignored, even spat on. The poorest of the poor have also lost old friends and family. And the poor know all about sin. They are poor because of sin, their own sin perhaps, but primarily because of the sins of others: greed, selfishness, exploitation, the failure of social and political systems.

Among the poor, let us admit, we feel uneasy, uncomfortable, nervous. This is so because in their poverty we ourselves are—implicitly— criticized. The condition of poverty is itself an incisive criticism of us and our national lifestyle. Without for a moment idealizing or romanti- cizing the poor, let us consider their gifts. Anyone who has ever spent time among the poor in any sort of collegiality will know just what their gifts are, so will those who have slept overnight in a shelter for the homeless or eaten meals in an urban soup kitchen. The poor, lacking pretense, help us to shed ours; having nothing, they make themselves freely available. They show concern for the stranger; they assist the afflicted. They understand suffering, loss, death, failure, and rejection, and they speak to the suffering, loss, death, failure, and rejection in our lives. Having no families of their own (or disorganized, fragmented ones), they are invariably interested in the families and children of others. Having little, they share much; having experienced lovelessness, they reach out in love, compassion, and gratitude. It is in these poor, wherever they are to be found, that God in the human face of Jesus is made manifest. It is here that God wants to be known and made known, here in the poor that God wants to be seen, experienced, adored, and followed.

> Jesus' God is the Father of infinite goodness who treasures the poor, the lost drachma, the stray sheep, the prodigal son. The worship that pleases God most is service rendered to others, and particularly to the lowest ones in whom God has hidden him- self. . . . We encounter God in the lives and faces of the humiliated and downtrodden. God chooses to be recognized and served in them. It is in the face of the afflicted that God chooses to make clear what he signifies. . . . They [the poor] are the great sacra- ment of God, the signs and instruments of authentic divine reality. If we do not share life with the oppressed, we do not share life with God.[8]

GOD'S "PREFERENTIAL OPTION FOR THE POOR"—OUR OPTION

The spirituality suggested in this chapter is one that seeks Jesus among the poor, because there God in Christ is made most manifest.

Building on the biblical imperative to serve the poor, the Latin American Roman Catholic bishops, meeting in Medellin, Columbia, in 1968, coined the phrase "preferential option for the poor" to describe the meaning of the service Christ intends his followers to pursue among the poor.[9] The preferential option for the poor was reinforced by the same group at Puebla in 1979.

> The Son of God demonstrated the grandeur of this commitment [to the poor] when he became a human being. For he identified himself with human beings by becoming one of them. He established solidarity with them and took up the situation in which they find themselves—in his birth and in his life, and particularly in his passion and death where poverty found its maximum expression (Phil. 2:5–8).
>
> For this reason alone, the poor merit preferential attention, whatever may be the moral or personal situation in which they find themselves. Made in the image and likeness of God (Gen. 1:26–28) to be his children, this image is dimmed and even defiled. That is why God takes on their defense and loves them (Matt. 5:45; James 2:5). That is why the poor are the first ones to whom Jesus' mission is directed (Luke 4:18–21), and why the evangelization of the poor is the supreme sign and proof of his mission (Luke 7:21–23).[10]

God's preferential option for the poor is a new phrase for an idea as old as belief itself. "The King will reply, 'I tell you, whenever you did this [fed the poor, gave drink, sheltered the homeless, clothed the naked, visited the sick and the imprisoned] for the least important of these brothers of mine, you did it for me' " (Matt. 25:40). "You did it for me" is the key phrase and the reason why we, too, in seeking and following Christ, must find him in the bruised and bloodied and battered and brutalized of our society.

Basic to belief is our full understanding and participation in God's preferential option for the poor. It is completely supported and affirmed by the early Church Fathers, whose convictions about Christian living continue to challenge and encourage contemporary Christians. We look to them today, knowing that they lived and wrote when the Gospel was still young and fresh and free of corruption and dilution. Early Christians did not divide the world between sacred and secular; they did not erect boundaries within which Christians were to carry on their activities; they sought to establish God's reign and his justice and love everywhere. They did not distinguish between theological and socioeconomic doctrines and theories, for they knew that

> if they went wrong in their fundamental conception of human and divine nature they would go wrong in the political and commercial theories which are the outcome of our fundamental conceptions about life.[11]

The Fathers looked to the Old Testament to verify their conviction that serving God is intimately mingled with issues of private property, ownership, and the seeking of justice for all people in temporal matters (Amos 5:21–24; Jer. 27:13–16; Isaiah 58:6–8) and that, if acted on, "He that giveth to the poor shall not want" (Prov. 28:27).

The *Didache,* written sometime in the second century, contains the first code of Christian morals; it is very clear about poverty and Christian sharing. Indeed, it is in sharing that one is led to genuine life. Conversely, not to share leads to death, for

> the Father wants his own gifts universally shared. Happy is the man who gives as the commandment bids.[12]

If our society does not question the right to hold private property, we would do well to note that the early Fathers did. They did so for three reasons: (1) the earth is the Lord's possession, not ours, and we are but stewards of the land; (2) because of the simple truth that if some possess private property while others do not, everyone will ultimately suffer and there will be fundamental inequality among persons; and (3) private ownership and possessions are impediments to belief.

Cyprian, Clement, Origen, and Irenaeus all took stands against private ownership, as did Polycarp. The Christian apologist Lactantius (c. 240–c. 310) wrote:

> Neither the Romans nor the Greeks were able to possess justice, because they kept men unequal with one another by many degrees, from the poor to the rich, from the lowly to the powerful, for where all are not equal, there is no equality; and inequality excludes justice. . . . This is perfect justice, which guards the human society; this is the greatest and truest fruit of riches: not to use wealth for one's personal pleasure, but for the welfare of many, not for one's own immediate enjoyment, but for justice, which alone perishes not.[13]

The fourth-century Church Fathers, both Latin and Greek, unanimously concurred: Athanasius, Basil, Gregory of Nazianzus, John Chrysostom,

Ambrose, Augustine of Hippo, Jerome and Gregory the Great.[14] Ambrose, bishop of Milan, was particularly direct in his passion for justice and the social message of the Gospel:

> The world was created for all men, and you, the rich minority, try to claim it for yourselves. Yes, not only the ownership of the earth, but heaven too, the air and the sea, is claimed for the use of the rich minority. This field which you enfold in your wide possessions, how many folk could it nourish? Surely the angels do not hold vaults of heaven divided up, as thou doest map the earth with thy boundary lines. . . .[15]

And let us not imagine that there is anyone who is exempt from sharing, for the poor themselves are bound to help others who are poor, fasting, if necessary, to provide for those needier than themselves:

> And if there is one poor and needy among them, and they have no extra means, they fast two or three days to provide the necessary food for the one in need.[16]

In a simple bamboo chapel in a teeming Guayaquil shantytown of ninety thousand in Ecuador, where there is neither running water nor sanitation facilities, where everybody is poor and the infant-mortality rate sky-high, I saw a collection box with the following inscription: *"Para los pobres. Ayudalos."* ("For the poor. Help them.")

And finally, however reluctant we may be to face issues of wealth and poverty as did the early Church Fathers, we know the truth—do we not—of John Chrysostom's words:

> If we lived as they [the earliest Christians] did we would soon convert the whole world, with no need of miracles at all.[17]

Dear reader, I am reproached by the biblical imperative, by the writings of the early Church Fathers, by my own words, for what is said we know to be true, and are we not, all of us, like the rich man Jesus talks about? Florence Nightingale, St. Francis of Assisi, Martin Luther King, Jr., Mother Teresa of Calcutta—they immediately leap to mind whenever we consider selfless service to the poor and oppressed. Why? Could it be because they are so few? Or do we know—in our heart of hearts—that these saints really live (or have lived) the lives all Christians are meant to live, doing for the poor what we too are meant to do? I have a dream that there might be a hundred thousand Florence Nighingales, a hundred thousand St. Francises, a hundred thousand Martin Luther Kings, a hundred thousand Mother Teresas scattered throughout all of God's earth and that they might be no more special than the kindly mayor of a small city, the faithful herdsman lovingly tending his flock in the lonely Afghanistan mountains, or the "Teacher of the Year" at the local elementary school. All Christians must show charity toward one another, and I am afraid that means *costly* charity, because the building blocks of God's kingdom in this world are acts of love and charity and their fruits: justice, generosity, long-suffering, hospitality, fortitude, faith. We who are materially advantaged must engage in lives of love among the poor, because there will our Lord be found.

In taking seriously the social message of the Gospel and its vital linking of liturgical and social action—particularly among the poor—the leaders of the Oxford Movement and contemporary liberation theologians are remarkably similar. E. B. Pusey, as quoted in chapter 6 ("Following Christ"), might well be Leonardo Boff; the words of Frank Weston, Anglican Bishop of Zanzibar in the 1920s, have the familiar ring of Gustavo Gutiérrez's. Weston directed the following remarks to his Anglo-Catholic colleagues:

> If you are prepared to fight for the right of adoring Jesus in his Blessed Sacrament, then you have got to come out from your Tabernacle and walk with Christ mystically present in you, out into the streets of this country, and find the same Jesus in the people of your cities and your villages. You cannot claim Jesus in the Tabernacle, if you do not pity Jesus in the slum. . . . And it is folly—it is madness—to suppose that you can worship Jesus in the Sacraments and Jesus on the throne of glory, when you are sweating him in the souls and bodies of his children. It cannot be done. . . . Go out and look for Jesus in the ragged, in the naked, in the oppressed and sweated, and in those who have lost hope . . . look for Jesus. And when you see him, gird yourselves with his towel and try to wash their feet.[18]

Gutiérrez speaks similar words, and with the same passion:

> As a sacramental community, the Church should signify in its own internal structures the salvation whose fulfillment it announces. . . . The place of the mission of the Church is where the celebration of the Lord's supper and the creation of human brotherhood are indissolubly joined. . . . Communion with God and others presupposes the abolition of all injustice and exploitation. This is expressed by the very fact that the Eucharist was instituted during a meal. For the Jews the common meal was a sign of brotherhood. It united the diners in a kind of sacred pact. Moreover, the bread and the wine are signs of brotherhood which at the same time suggest the gift of creation. The objects used in the Eucharist

themselves recall that brotherhood is rooted in God's will to give the goods of this earth to all people so that they might build a more human world.[19]

But unless the Church is willing to make profound changes in its ecclesial structures, Christians of advantage will simply patronize the poor by exploiting them for their own spiritual needs. Poor people always have been thus misused. That they have been used for the material gain of others is terrible; it would be horrifying if they were also to be used for the spiritual benefit of others. To preclude such exploitation, the poor themselves ought to be the agents of their own pastoral activity; indeed, they could become the people to lead in the transformation of the Church.

> The marginated and the dispossessed still do not have their own voice in the Church of him who came to the world especially for them. Their real presence in the Church would work a profound transformation in its structures, its values, and its actions.[20]

If Christ is really our model and if we honestly want to follow him by imitating him in our own lives, we will be challenged to say, with Jesus and Isaiah, "The spirit of the Lord is upon me, because God has chosen me to bring good news to the poor. God has sent me to proclaim liberty to the captives and recovery of sight to the blind, to set free the oppressed, and announce that the time has come when the Lord will save his people" (Luke 4:18–19). And most of all we are challenged to *do* as Jesus and Isaiah did, for we recall John's words, "My children, our love should not be just words and talk; it must be true love which shows itself in action" (1 John 3:18). To act on the truth of the Gospel and its social implications, as stressed as Puebla, would mean nothing less than the conversion of the whole Church, for

> service to them [the poor] calls for constant conversion and purification among all Christians. That must be done if we are to achieve fuller identification each day with the poor Christ and our own poor.[21]

God's preferential option for the poor is our option; it is not merely the best way to follow Jesus, it is the only way that leads to abundant life.

CHAPTER 10

DO THIS IN REMEMBRANCE OF ME

> The separation today between piety and action seems
> as great as ever, and one of the most urgent problems
> which a renewed liturgical theology must address.
>
> —Louis Weil,
> *Sacraments and Liturgy*

LIFE COMING TO LITURGY

Liturgy is public service done for others; it is primarily action, not words. It is like lungs, breathing not for themselves but for the whole organism; it is like the heart, pumping life-giving blood into every cell of the body. All of life ought to find expression in liturgy, and all liturgy ought to reflect every aspect of life. Derived from two Greek words, *laos* (people) and *ergon* (work), liturgy, properly understood, is the "work of the people." In its original, secular context the term suggested public works. As John Robinson explains, it comes from the realm of municipal affairs. In ancient Greece, citizens were required to exercise responsibility for certain public works—such as the building and maintaining of roads, the repair of civil buildings and docks—public works done for the welfare of all citizens and their cities.[1]

The Holy Communion—that is, God's holy community—ought to express every aspect of human community while being in itself a foretaste of God's heavenly community. In its structure and make-up it ought to express the peace, the love, the justice, the forebearance, the pity, the generosity of God—a microcosm of all God proclaims through the Gospel. All ministry is liturgy, and liturgy is public affairs, not private devotions. According to Louis Weil,

> the authentic liturgical act is not a luxury for the Church. It is decisive, critical and formative; it is the bloodstream of the Body of Christ. It is not a question merely of effective or well-planned ritual. It is an act which reveals what the Church is.[2]

It is also an act that reveals what God is. The Eucharist, the liturgical service that is the primary subject of this chapter, ought—in every way— to be what it is and to do what it says, for we recall Christ's words in the Eucharistic Prayer (prayer of consecration), when the president prays over the bread and wine, saying: "This is my Body which is given for you. *Do this* [italics mine] for the remembrance of me." Christ's words are not "say this," "think this," "consider this," or even "pray about this"; they are simply the command: *"Do this."*

Do what? Do as Christ did; replicate in our day the ministry he practiced in his.

Twenty-five years ago John Robinson, the Anglican bishop of Woolwich famous for his controversial book *Honest to God,* published another book, *Liturgy Coming to Life,* (it was little noticed by comparison). It was an apt title, describing both the process of Eucharistic liturgical reform that brings the rite to life and the ways in which the four actions of the Eucharist—taking, blessing, breaking, sharing—ought to be lived by Christians participating fully in the life of the world beyond the parish walls.[3] But for that to occur as God intends, life—the authentic life of the community—in all its pain, fullness, joy, suffering, and ambiguity— must come to the liturgy and there be transformed into a new world and sent out to transform the old.

The liturgists who have painstakingly revised the Eucharistic liturgies of the major denominations over the past two dozen years have done excellent work. They have successfully brought the liturgy to the people, making it intimate; they have made possible an increase in numbers of official participants, they have revised archaic language, they have peeled away unnecessary layers and thoroughly grounded the rite in the traditions of the earliest Christian communities. Make no mistake: The crucial importance of these revised rites cannot be overestimated; they have contributed greatly to keeping countless socially active Christians from washing their hands of the official Church because of its irrelevancy. In all honesty, however, must we not acknowledge that, improved as these rites are, something of major importance is still missing?

While writing this chapter, I paused to make my family's weekly bread, and it prompted me to reflect on the arts of bread baking and of building up the body of Christ. The flour is the best on the market; according to the package label, it is "unbleached forever, all purpose, enriched, presifted." It contains "no bleaching agents or preservatives." But good as it is, it will not turn into bread without yeast. Why yeast? Yeast is just a name for a humble organism that, added to the bowl of flour, causes fermentation, enticing the lifeless flour to bubble and rise, making possible in several hours a half dozen high, rounded, beautifully shaped loaves. As I kneaded the yeast into the flour, a thought disturbed me: Are not Eucharistic rites like just so much flour, yes even flour of the best quality—nice, pure, good, enriched—rites that will not be transformed into loaves, loaves that will never feed and nourish without the common agent of yeast? Is not the yeast like the teeming masses of God's world? Inelegant as it is, yeast is required to make the flour come alive; without it the flour is dead, it will not turn into bread, it will never *do* anything but *be* a lifeless mass.

So often our religious ceremonies are devoid of the essential yeast of life, of the power that would truly feed the people and nourish God's creation. We feel the lack of nourishing liturgy and perhaps we identify with Annie Dillard, young lady of American letters, who has said,

> I often think of the set pieces of liturgy as certain words which people have successfully addressed to God without getting killed. In the high churches they saunter through the liturgy like Mohawks along a strand of scaffolding who have long since forgotten their danger.[4]

LITURGY WITHOUT LIFE IS A LIE

Life *must* come to liturgy as the yeast of this world must come to the flour, which is the Church; we cannot continue to "saunter through the liturgy like Mohawks along a strand of scaffolding. . . ." And let us get the order right: The life of the world comes *before* the liturgy of the Church, *not* the converse, for the destiny of the human community is dependent on just and cordial relations between persons. Righting such relations takes precedence over strictly religious rites. Christ certainly put community and right relations before worship, for he was thoroughly outspoken in declaring that grievances between persons ought to be settled before entering into worship: "So if you are offering your gift at the altar, and there remember that your brother has something against you, leave your gift before the altar and go; first be reconciled to your brother, and then come and offer your gift" (Matt. 5:23–25). And recalling the warning of the Old Testament prophet Amos, we are reminded of God's priorities: "I hate and despise your feasts and I take no delight in your solemn assemblies. Even though you offer me your burnt offerings and cereal offerings, I will not accept them, and the peace offerings of your fatted beasts I will not look upon. Take away the noise of your songs; to the melody of the harp I will not listen. But let justice roll down like waters, and righteousness like an everlasting stream" (Amos 5:21–24).

Liturgy is a lie and a deceit (some even have suggested it is demonic) that does not reflect God's kingdom and God's liberation, which the Gospel announces. In 1925 Geoffrey Studdert Kennedy declared:

> Where worship is divorced from work, and God's presence in the sanctuary from his presence in the street, we run the deadly danger of localizing God, and our sacraments may be turned into sin. If the sacrament is to take its proper place as the central act of Christian worship, Christian people must learn to see in it the whole purpose and meaning of their daily work.[5]

Contemporary Church leaders and liturgists would agree (and some would contend) that the sacraments are in crisis because it is so often the case that the reality of the Eucharistic words is simply not borne out in the actions of God's people. Tissa Balasuriya, a Sri Lankan Roman Catholic liturgist, said:

> The Eucharist is in captivity. It is dominated by persons who do not experience oppression in their own selves. Even within the poor countries, the Church leaders generally belong to the side of the affluent elite. The Eucharist will not be liberated to its mission so long as the churches are captive within the world's power establishments. The Eucharist has to be liberative; it should lead to sharing and genuine love. But in its social impact it fails to do so. It has been interpreted conservatively, rigidly, and formally.[6]

Juan Luis Segundo of Uruguay has stressed the conditions under which the sacraments will be "efficacious." In reference to the Eucharist, he said:

> The sacraments will be valid and efficacious, as Christ intended, to the extent that they are a consciousness-raising and motivating celebration of man's liberative action in history. That does not reduce them to a merely human gesture. God is operative in them, but his activity consists in working through the praxis of man. Hence it condenses in the sacramental celebration where man intensifies his conscious awareness of the impact and liberative force of his action. Where this does not happen, there efficacious truth and true efficacy will be missing—no matter how perfect the rite is.[7]

Louis Weil, liturgist of the American Episcopal Church, is somewhat less harsh. Nonetheless, in *Sacraments and Liturgy* he criticizes the Church for tolerating, and even subtly promoting, an individualized piety inherited from the Middle Ages, when overbearing clericalism led to the development of a passive laity. It was a piety, still alive and well today, in which the realities of the world were held at arm's length, escape from the world was embraced, and sacraments were more like sedatives than seeds of celebration.[8] He says:

Our inherited attitude towards the liturgical act reflects a kind of schizoid state. We hear, but do not really *hear*. The liturgy is an encapsulated experience, entered into in isolation from real human experiences. It does not connect with the real world because it has been shaped by a piety which is often consciously an escape from the pressures of the real world. Liturgical time is seen as "holy time" working according to its own laws, and feeding our hunger and thirst for God. But it does not connect for the great majority of our people with the real choices of daily life.[9]

Finally, the sharpest criticism comes from Paul Gibson, who, in a paper presented to the cathedral deans of the Anglican Church of Canada, asserted:

The liturgy is the point at which shalom (or kingdom, whichever you prefer) is symbolized and therefore made available, to redeem the past and transform the present for the sake of the future. Liturgy without justice and peace is deformed and if it reinforces disinterest in justice and peace it is demonic.[10]

The Eucharist loses its meaning, its power, its effect, when its celebrants are closed to their neighbors, insensitive to injustice, and little bothered by the poverty and the distress of God's children on the edges of existence. As Segundo has so rightly cautioned:

There are times when it seems that our yearning and zeal for ritual and liturgical renewal is a superficial way of solving a much deeper problem: the problem of community. Liturgical reform will not resolve the crisis. Its real and undeniable usefulness may in fact be to heighten it. For with each passing day the absence of authentic Christian community will become even clearer. Only the intrinsic and functional coherence of the latter will enable us to rediscover and live the mystery embedded in the sacramental signs.[11]

Studdert Kennedy would concur, for he said:

The Christian life of devotion and the Christian ideal of community are inextricably bound up with one another, and stand and fall together. . . . When that sacrament [of the breaking of the bread] is divorced from the dream of a Christian social order, it is deprived of its true significance. If we cut off that bread which is his body from all connection with our daily bread, and the means whereby we earn it; if we delcare that he is present in the Bread of the sanctuary, but absent from the bread of the street—we deny the truth of the incarnation. We deny that "The WORD became flesh through whom all things were made and without whom nothing was made that was made."[12]

Just as the bread of life is shared abundantly and unconditionally in the Eucharist, so must bread be shared abundantly and unconditionally with all who are hungry. It is crucial that Christians make the connection between the Eucharistic meal and any other meal. We cannot share the one without also sharing the other. Liturgy detached from the life of the world is a lie; it is like a short circuit, electricity that will not yield light, like yeastless flour that will not make bread. Detached, liturgy is a lie; it belies the life of the one who is the life and light of the world—Jesus Christ. Without that vital linkage, liturgical reform is merely the meaningless moving of powerless pawns on an ecclesiastical chessboard.

LITURGY COMING TO LIFE

Worship will be authentic only inasmuch as the community of worshipers allows itself to be transformed by the servant Jesus and his cross. Liturgy will come to life to the extent that the life of this world comes to the liturgy, giving it human form, breathing into it God's breath of life. And in that liturgy is, as John Robinson has said, "the great workshop of the new world,"[13] *everything* of the life of this world, everything that converges in our personal and corporate lives must be gathered together and offered in the Eucharist. As the bread is gathered and offered in the fourfold action of the Eucharist—taking, blessing, breaking, sharing—so these liturgical acts must become the symbols of our lives and the life of the world. In them we ask the Lord to *take* us and all of our lives as his own, forever; to *bless,* for we recall that "God saw everything that he had made, and behold, it was very good" (Gen. 1:31); to *break,* so that, broken, we can be remade more nearly as Christ's children, made whole so we can work to make his creation whole. Finally, we take back our lives brought to the liturgy—lives that have been returned to us renewed, blessed, broken, made whole—so we can then *share* them generously for the transformation of God's world. This effect of the liturgy is, as Segundo has explained, the

> rhythmic dialectical dimension of social and historical activity. It is the community's way of reactivating and deepening our interpretation of, and commitment to, the historical process geared towards man's liberation.[14]

No concern is too small to be brought to the Eucharist, no issue too large. The sighs of the dying, the worries of the weary, the joys of the just graduated or married or the longings of citizens for a just society, belong there, as does our dread of nuclear holocaust, our pity for the starving in Africa, our distress over Central American unrest and all manner of environmental, social, and political issues. Our temptation, however, is to give priority to our personal concerns, sometimes neglecting altogether the pressing social issues of our times. In most congregations, people's free intercessions are full of prayers for the sick and dying and very meager with prayers for the social order. The priority of our prayers must be reversed, for unless we put the social order first there will, in time, be no social order and nothing personal to pray for, because there will be no one on the face of the earth.

Two commissions of the Episcopal Church (the Standing Commission on Metropolitan Affairs and the Standing Commission on World Mission) have written a "Common Statement" for consideration by the 1985 General Convention of the Church. It identifies current trends and issues that ought to be addressed by the Church and, I would add, brought into the life of the Eucharist:

> Unprecedented developments are transforming global society; together they comprise a challenge and an opportunity that is massive. The kind of response that is made will determine the character of global society for centuries to come. Environmental, resource, and population stresses are intensifying and will increasingly determine the quality of human life on our planet. These stresses are already severe enough to deny many millions of people basic needs of food, shelter, health and jobs, or any hope of betterment. At the same time the earth's carrying capacity—the ability of biological systems to provide resources for human needs— is eroding.
>
> If these trends are to be altered and the problems diminished, vigorous new initiatives will be required to meet human needs while protecting and restoring the earth's capacity to support life.[15]

The issues cited in the "Common Statement" are those of justice, peace, and the environment. I can do no better than simply to repeat them because, in my opinion, they serve as an outline of the global character of Christian prayer that ought to find its way into the liturgy:

Issues of Justice:

Justice is the dominant issue of our day. Our faith teaches that the creation is good and that human beings have the right to basic needs. In our Baptismal Covenant we affirm that we will "strive for justice and peace among all people, and respect the dignity of every human being." In faithfulness to that promise, we proclaim these Gospel values: medical care, education, free communication, access to work, religious freedom, and civil rights.

Only as the Church joins in the struggle for the fulfillment of these values will it be faithful to its call to bring good news to the poor; to proclaim liberty to the captives; to set free the oppressed" (Isaiah 61:1–2; Luke 4:16).

Issues of Peace:

Among the issues of peace, we proclaim the following:

1) Nuclear disarmament: The threat of nuclear holocaust demands priority attention from the Christian Church. A holocaust would make mockery of the Church's effort to deal with any other issue. A process leading to nuclear disarmament offers the only alternative to an eventual holocaust.

2) Reconciliation of differences among nations. . . .

3) Equitable distribution of resources. Humankind urgently needs international means to reduce conflict over inequities of access to fundamental necessities of life.

Issues of the Environment:

There can be neither peace nor justice as long as there are drastic differences in access to food, water and energy among the people of the earth. At the Eucharist we pray that our Lord will "give us all a reverence for the earth as God's own creation," and that "we may use its resources rightly in the service of others and to God's honor and glory." The care of "this fragile planet, our island home" (from Eucharistic Prayer C) is part of the call to the Church.

Among the most serious issues affecting the climate for a just and peaceful society are desertification, as an area the size of the State of Maine turns to desert every year; deforestation, because an increasingly poor people use forests for fuel; soil erosion caused by deforestation, increased salinity, and lack of affordable fertilizers; pollution of water and air, from spilled chemicals, acid rain, carbon dioxide, pesticides; declining water supplies; the ambiguous legacy of nuclear power [nuclear refuse dumps, etc.]; and the responsible use of outer space.[16]

Finally, the "Common Statement" reminds us that

Christ is sending us into the world to be practitioners of that compassionate discipleship which is the essence of Christian living. . . . We are called to nothing less than to follow Christ and lead others to him. . . . We are called by the Holy Spirit to daring visions and bold actions. We are being sent to participate in revealing to the world the transformation of *what is* into what God has shown in Christ *can and ought to be.*[17]

Liturgy will come to life as the life of this world comes more and more into the liturgy of the Church; it will come to life as all of the world's affairs are brought into Christ's presence and there be taken, blessed, broken, transformed by his action—and then shared absolutely, abundantly, and unconditionally in society.

Before closing, let me add that the structure of our worship must, in every way, conform to the ideals of the kind of loving, just, and moral society the liturgy suggests. As Paul Gibson wrote:

> The style of the assembly may be more important than the words that are said. The assembly itself must be seen and felt to be a just society, a society in which every member is valued and each member group is adequately represented. A liturgy in which some members are treated as unimportant or in which women, or black people, or children, or the aged, are marginalized, or which is dominated rather than led by the clergy, is not a schoolhouse of the kingdom.[18]

The language, the music, the colors of our culture and environment should be a part of our worship spaces and liturgical forms, just as art, music, and artifacts contribute to making us who we are. To enter some preceived "holy life" suspended in time and space, Christians for too long have left "real life" at the lych gate. Unless our meeting places reflect what and who we are, they will be but ecclesiastical museums where fossilized Christian liturgy is seen as some sort of other worldly object rather than an action to be lived by all. The familiar architectural axiom that "form follows function" must apply not only to the design of our worship spaces but to the shaping of our liturgy.

The steel band, the rock band, the drum that beats with the heartbeat of the people, must be made part of Christian worship. Paintings, sculpture—all the artforms of the people—ought to be included. The liturgy ought to be in the common language, the tongue in which we speak to our beloveds, our children, our colleagues and neighbors.

The bread we offer at the Eucharist ought to be that which comes from our ovens, our family dining tables. And when the liturgical celebration is finished, let us take the extra bread out of the church and into the streets and marketplaces and there feed the hungry and continue the Eucharist, just as the first generations of Christians did. And let Eucharistic wine be the product of local vineyards; it represents the work of nature and of human hands. Let us not put it away as a "reserved sacrament," as if it were some sort of magical tonic only the presbyter is holy enough to touch. No, let us take the wine away from our altars and carry it into our cities and towns, into the countryside, there to be abundantly shared with everyone who thirsts.

There are already some encouraging signs that the liturgy is coming to life. Amidst the bloodshed, brutality, and martyrdom in Central and South America, new life is arising from Church communities. In African village after African village—in the midst of wrenching poverty—whole communities are converting to Christ and thousands of new Christians are living the renascent liturgy. Liturgy will come to life in the developed world, too, if we but dare to *do this*—do Christ's ministry—in our day as he did in his.

> The Holy Communion is the great workshop of the new world, where the "we who are many" are recreated as the true, the new community in Christ. And the holy community known at the liturgy is the norm of what has to be made true of all society. Here indeed is the classless society in which there is neither Jew nor Greek, male nor female, bond nor free. We are not called to "bring in" the kingdom of God, but to bring it out from where we have known it. Our task is not to "build" what does not yet exist, but to "build up" what is already there, that cell of the new society which is present wherever two or three are gathered in Christ's name. The Communion is social dynamite if we really take seriously the pattern of community known at the altar. We have to discover . . . *the absolutely unconditional sharing of bread.*[19]

When we do so, liturgy will indeed come to life and true life will come to liturgy.

CHAPTER 11

BUILDING UP THE BODY OF CHRIST

Tell these dry bones to listen to the word of the Lord.
Tell them that I, the Sovereign Lord, am saying to them:
I am going to put breath into you and bring you back
to life. I will give you sinews and muscles. . . .

—Ezekiel 37:4–6

"Can these dry bones live?" (Ezek. 37:3). The Lord's question to the Old Testament prophet Ezekiel is also our question: Can these dry bones—the skeleton that is the Church—live? Can it have sinews and muscles? Can the head be connected to the body, the arms and legs to the trunk, can the hands and feet, the fingers and toes be fitted together in perfect harmony according to their functions? And can this body be clothed in human flesh that is also the flesh of Christ? Can it have a stout heart to pump the blood of life into every limb and every cell? Can it have lungs to breathe fresh air—the breath of God's life—throughout the organism? Can its senses be tuned to pick up the touch, the tempo, the taste, the texture of the environment and to communicate those stimuli to the heart of the body? Can the body's eyes see the world through God's eyes; can its ears hear the world with God's ears; can its mouth speak to the world in God's voice?

For *the* Christian action, that *par excellence* which mediates Christ's saving work in the world is, always and essentially, the action of *Christ in his body.* This is what the Church, as the body of Christ, exists to do for the world. This is our "liturgy," the piece of public work laid upon us within the world as citizens of God's commonwealth.[1]

Ezekiel's answer to the Lord's question was: "O Lord God, Thou knowest" (Ezek. 37:4). As with Ezekiel in his day, so with us in ours.

The Lord alone knows whether his body—the Church—can live and flourish. Like Ezekiel, we do not know the answer to God's question. There are, however, some things we do know about the body: The better all its parts are joined, the better the body will function. "Christ is like a single body which has many parts; it is still one body, even though it is made up of different parts. In the same way, all of us . . . have been baptized into the one body by the same Spirit, and we have all been given one Spirit to drink" (1 Cor. 12:12–13).

I like the biblical metaphor of the human body and the Church as the body of Christ. Just as the human body is one organism composed of many parts—all crucial to its proper functioning—so the Church is a dynamic organism that functions best when all its parts are joined and well harmonized.

A body can function without an arm or a leg, or with paralyzed limbs; it can function with weak lungs and heart disease. Bodies with impaired hearing and vision can still hear and see. A less than complete or poorly conditioned body can and does function, it can "get by." The Church is such a body; it has been "getting by" for most of its long life. It has not been a unified and harmoniously operating organism. An arm has, at times, forgotten about—or thought it could manage without—the rest of the body; the body has not had buoyant lungs and a clear voice. Parts of the body have been paralyzed. It has often been deaf and short-sighted; its dulled senses have not felt and perceived with acuity. Most of all, the body of the Church has not had a big enough, or a robust enough, heart.

Part of my intention for this book has been to illustrate some of the ways the body of Christ's Church has failed to function, or has functioned inadequately.

The first and most serious injury to the body was the cutting off—the amputation, if you will—of the clergy from the rest of the body, the laity of the Church. This has led to other less radical amputations: distinct clerical spirituality; distinct ways of participating in the liturgy, depending on whether one is lay or ordained; distinct clerical lifestyles and dress. There have also been divisions—between sacred and secular, wealth and poverty, ideal and practice, what the Church says and what it does, justice and injustice, service among Church members and service in God's world, the contemplative and the activist members of the body. Whole limbs of the Church—the lay limb in particular—have been paralyzed by the sluggishness and malfunctioning of the body as a whole. Finally, God's body the Church, in its fragmented state, has been presumptuous enough to conduct itself as if it could exist independently of, and at times oblivious to, the environment of which it is an organic part.

Stating the condition of God's body the Church is not a matter of assigning blame; no specific person or set of events or circumstances caused the dis-ease. And certainly the disease has taken centuries to develop into its present condition. Part of the Church's condition is that it has been in it for so long that most of its parts (members) have forgotten (if they ever knew) what the body could feel like if it were to function healthily, harmoniously, and to capacity.

This book has been, in a way, a physical, social, and spiritual examination of the body we call Christ's Church. It has been a general examination by a general practitioner of the faith. We have begun to examine some of the diseases and conditions currently affecting the Church: the demise of the idea of the priesthood of all believers and the development of the clericalized Church, the many ways members of the body reflect on and interpret God's revelation (spirituality and theology), calendars of saints, the liturgy. This examination has, I hope, shed some light on how some of the conditions evolved and, where possible, has suggested a few remedies.

Because the Church is a two-thousand-year-old body and its dis-eases and conditions did not develop overnight, its healing cannot be accomplished overnight or with a few glib paragraphs and chapters. As for any body in which disease is found, it is prudent to get a "second opinion." The body of the Church needs second, third, and fourth opinions. It needs close-up and thorough examinations by other general practitioners in the healing arts of faith and by specialists as well.

As the examination of the patient (the Church) continues, one finds many aspects of the body's life (in addition to those discussed in the preceding chapters) that future physicians of the faith ought to examine. They need to come to a renewed understanding of the extent and character of God's activity in the world and of the nature of sacredness. Christians need to examine issues of wealth and poverty, and they ought to take a fresh look at ministry, both lay and ordained.

A RENEWED SENSE OF GOD'S ALL-EMBRACING ACTIVITY IN THE WORLD

God is God of creation, Lord of the earth; he made all and is in, under, and above all. No area of creation is too remote, no person beyond the reach of his saving embrace. "God looked at *everything* he had made, and he was very pleased" (Gen. 1:31a); "For God loved the *world* so much that he gave his only Son" (John 3:16a); "For in Christ God reconciled the *world* to himself" (2 Cor. 5:19).

There is an arrogance among Christians that equates God's activity with service in the institutional Church and that measures religious commitment exclusively by institutional service. The more committees Church people belong to or chair, the more important the institutional decisions they make, the more they are at the service of the ordained ministers of the Church, the more lessons they read at public worship, the more prayers they recite—the better the Christians they are considered to be. And there is a kind of spiritual one-up-manship by which those caught up in these churchly activities quietly discriminate against those who are not. By and large, unless a layperson has an exceptional job of obvious Christian service in the community, such as that of the only town doctor or the beloved village schoolmaster, nothing he or she does in the way of Christian service will be so much as noticed—no less supported or affirmed—by his or her congregation. Christian service is equated with service within the institutional structures of the Church.

How easily we forget that God came, first and foremost, to save the world, not the Church, and that the Church is not a world unto itself but a body that ought to be in service to the world. Our God is not small, but our conception of God is. The idea that there can be no salvation outside the Church came into sharpest focus during the Middle Ages, when "to be for or against Christ came to be fully identified with being for or against the Church."[2] This ecclesiocentric perspective and its legacy— still very much evident in the Church—have, however subtly, shaped the whole mission and ministry of the Church and undermined the universality of Christ's mission. They have accentuated obedience to the institution, passivity in the general body, competition among leading lay members; they have made some Christians strident and judgmental. They have stressed "we" within the Church structures, "they" and "them" outside them; "us" within Church walls, "the other" beyond them. Christians have looked down on people outside their ranks, those they ought lovingly to have served. But, according to Bonhoeffer:

> She [the Church] must take her part in the social life of the world, not lording it over men, but helping and serving them. . . . And in particular our own Church will have to take a strong line with the blasphemies of the *hybris,* power-worship, envy and humbug, for these are the roots of evil.[3]

Competition among members, inwardness, a diminished and narrow interpretation of God's all-embracing ministry and mission in the world must stop, for the Church is in a strait jacket and the body is paralyzed. As Gutiérrez wrote:

The Church must cease considering itself as the exclusive place of salvation and orient itself towards a new and radical service of people.[4]

A RESTORED PERSPECTIVE ON SACRED AND SECULAR

Some Christians creep around the chancel and tiptoe in the sanctuary; they speak in hushed voices as if they might disturb the sleeping God behind the sacristy door. Though there is nothing wrong with reverence, this kind of holy tiptoeing is usually characteristic of one who says, "God is to be found here in the Church," implying that God is not to be found elsewhere. Presbyters kissing the vestments they wear in services but failing to embrace God in the people beyond the sanctuary, the kissing of bishops' rings, the bowing in reverence before crosses while ignoring the persons who live the crucified Christ in their lives, carrying within themselves his cross—these customs are indicative of a misplaced sense of what is sacred and what is not, of a distorted geography as to where the holy is and is not to be found. A misplaced sense of the sacred is one of the results of the loss of a cosmic view of God's creation. For if we believe that salvation is possible only through the Church, it follows that the sacred, the holy, is to be found primarily within church buildings. It makes sense, then, that Christians appear to revere anything in church with a holy look to it.

I simply do not see Christians according the same consideration and respect to persons they feel toward inanimate religious objects in religious buildings. As Ecuador's Bishop Leonidas Proaño put it:

> We must ask ourselves whether we perhaps do not show greater respect to images made of wood than to human beings who are living images of God. We must ask ourselves whether we are not more courteous to images than to human beings who are sunk in ignorance, sorrow, poverty, and slavery.[5]

Just think of it: If Christians had the same sense of *all* space, not just church (building) space, as holy, our fragile planet would be treated with such respect that it would suffer no polluted land, waters, or air. The terms "desertification" and "deforestation" would be unknown, and the ugly scars of strip mining would be nonexistent.

Because God created the world and declared it good, nothing ought to be secular, no place in creation where the holy is not to be found. An ancient text cites one of Jesus' little-known sayings: "Lift a stone and I am under it; split a log and I am within it."[6]

If Christians had the same reverence for all persons as they have for religious objects in church buildings, they would not tolerate the poverty, oppression, and injustice visited on some persons in God's creation by others, for God loved us so much that he became a person in Jesus Christ, a person who took on our flesh, who lived among us and died for us, who was in every way a person for others. Robert Hovda reminds us:

> The sacredness of public worship [in church buildings] does not derive from the place of worship, nor from the furnishings or objects used in worship. Sacredness derives from the Christian assembly and its liturgical action.[7]

Let us allow God to expand our vision, to help us honor all of his creation as sacred, all of his creatures as holy, and let us affirm with John Robinson that:

> For Christianity, the holy is the depth of the common, just as the secular is not a godless section of life, but the world (God's world for which Christ died). . . .[8]

CHRISTIANS AND ISSUES OF WEALTH AND POVERTY

The Church Fathers were wise to see that all property and goods were held in common for the common good. Throughout the ages nations' desire for land, resources, and other material goods have led to heroic explorations and worldwide colonial expansion. The latter has resulted in war, bloodshed, the destruction of culture, and genocide. Individuals have been no less greedy. They have cleared the land and uprooted its prior inhabitants; they have "gentrified" urban slums, sometimes condemning the former slum dwellers to homelessness. Homelessness has now become a way of life to billions of people the world over.

In contemporary society the holding of private property is unquestioned. It is regarded as a right, and there are all sorts of government incentives, including a federal income tax that heavily favors home buyers and owners, to help people buy private homes. But what happens to all those who, despite federal help, cannot begin to afford even the most modest house?

Certainly it is unrealistic to imagine Christians would sell everything and live communally, as did the early Church Fathers (although some have done, and are doing, just that). And surely not everyone is inclined to join a monastery. (In any case, most monasteries have substantial property holdings as well as invested assets.)

It does seem reasonable to suggest, however, that it is high time for Christians to look at their assets and to determine what land and housing they need to fulfill their basic needs. How, for example, can any Christian honestly justify owning a vacation home in addition to a permanent residence when so many of God's children have no homes? It took but one brief visit to a Santo Domingo barrio to impress on me just how little housing people need and, by contrast, how much housing space and land most of us in the developed world *think* we need. Obviously farmers and ranchers require hundreds of acres for their crops and livestock, but perhaps two acres of land is too much property for a family of four, and seven rooms too much house for a retired couple. But we know that if the small family or the elderly couple were to vacate their ample homes, the liberated space would not automatically be made available to the unemployed mother with six children eking out an existence in a cramped urban apartment. So the problem is not merely one of land and housing; it is primarily one of the equitable distribution of property. People need what they need, and beyond that we all ought to look very critically at our property and, of course, our other possessions as well.

If we do not yet have the will or the power to insist on governmentally controlled, equitable distribution of housing throughout the country, there is still a great deal we as individuals can and ought to do. At the least, consider for a moment how much money could be saved and given to the poor if we were to live according to our actual needs rather than according to the usual considerations that determine how and where we live and the amounts and kinds of property we own. Issues of wealth and property are complex, but the dictates of our conscience and the demands of the Gospel urge us to face them.

It is an encouraging sign that some branches of the institutional Church are beginning to assess their assets in light of human need in society. They know that a Church encumbered by the weight of its property can hardly expect to serve with any sort of integrity a society where so many of God's children live in dire poverty. To the degree that the Church is encumbered by its property and wealth its ministry in the world will also be encumbered. When Bonhoeffer reflected on these matters from his prison cell, he declared:

> The Church is her true self only when she exists for humanity. As a fresh start she should give away her endowments to the poor and needy.[9]

St. Francis would agree.

In a 1984 pastoral letter to the clergy in the New Zealand diocese of

Auckland, the archbishop of New Zealand, Paul Reeves, and the other two bishops said:

> The Church is an institution which has material resources. Therefore every committee, vestry or trust board when it is making a decision about Church property or money must look not only to the needs of the Church but also at the human needs in the wider community. They should seek ways to share what they have with people who have little. . . . Will it be possible for the Church to transfer more of its resources to those who urgently need them? As a Church we will not find this easy. We are not accustomed to giving our material assets away. But we can't afford to end up like the well-intentioned, rich young man who when he was challenged to give what he had to the poor "went away sorrowful; for he had great possessions" (Matt. 19:16–22). These are hard issues but we must face them.[10]

Amen.

THE PRIME MINISTERS OF THE CHURCH . . .

The laity are the prime ministers of the Church. They are the normative Christians, the means through whom Christ enters the world and participates in every aspect of human activity. They are Christ's hands and feet and heart and mind. They are the human face of God; they are the doorways of his extravagant love; they are the instruments of his peace, his justice, his truth and equity, his forbearance, long-suffering hope and comfort, and—yes—joy.

Many if not most Christians are only dimly aware—if aware at all—of the essential ways in which they represent Christ in the world. I heartily agree with Leonardo Boff, who has maintained that whenever humanity is open to God and fellow persons, whenever true self-giving love exists and selfishness is overcome, and whenever human beings seek justice, peace, and forgiveness, then true Christianity emerges and acts in human history.[11]

Few would deny that Christ was being served as dozens of rock-music stars performed at Live Aid, a dazzling, sixteen-hour, live televised concert filmed in two locations on two continents and beamed by satellite to one hundred fifty nations—all for the benefit of the millions of people starving in Africa. It was either watched or listened to by one in five persons on the planet. Who would deny that Christ was present or that the $70 million raised for the cause was but a massive outpouring of generosity on the part of all involved, stars and spectators alike? And whether he was conscious of it or not (it doesn't really matter, does it?), who would deny that Christ's hand was very much on Bob Geldof, the concert's organizer? Prior to the Live Aid Concert, Geldof, leader of the Boomtown Rats band, was mainly known as the performer who brought live rats onto the concert stage and released them into the audience at the show's end. Now the governments of several nations have nominated him for the Nobel Peace Prize and in England he has been affectionately nicknamed "Saint Bob." Few would deny that on that midsummer day in 1985 egoism was overcome as rock stars (and the rest of the world, it seemed) gathered in a campaign for the relief of hunger and that, throughout the entire effort, Christ was being served.

The Live Aid Concert was but one dramatic example of the way God acts on the world stage. He also acts through all of us on our stages, on the stages where we live and move and conduct our daily lives and affairs. And with us, just as with the billions of persons caught up in the concert for the relief of African hunger, we may not be conscious of God acting through us. It is better, of course, if we *are* aware of it, but whether or not we are, God decidedly does work through us to accomplish the goals of the Gospel.

This is the primary ministry of the laity: living Christ's mission in the world. The Puebla Document stated:

> It is in the world that the laity find their specific field of activity. Through the witness of their lives, timely speaking out, and concrete action, the laity have the responsibility of giving order to temporal realities and placing them in the service of establishing God's Kingdom.[12]

And according to Gutiérrez:

> In his temporal endeavors, the layman will seek to create with other men, Christian or not, a more just and human society; he will be well aware that in so doing he is ultimately building up a society in which man will be able to respond freely to the call of God.[13]

If the laity of Christ's Church are intentionally to regain their central place in the body as its prime ministers, they will have to put the clergy in their place. The clergy, after all, have very effectively kept the laity in their place for hundreds of years and have frustrated and blocked them in the rightful exercise of their primary ministries. But enough is enough! The time has arrived for the laity to turn the tables. The time has arrived for the Church's prime ministers to act in every way as if they were the primary ministers they are, and for them graciously to accept, celebrate, and act on the primacy of their ministries. The time has arrived for the laity to say yes to the important ministry into which they are being led and to say no to all who would continue to usurp their crucial role.

When we use bodily imagery to describe ministry, as did St. Paul and the early Christians, it is easy to understand it as a matter of the functioning of the various parts of the body. We do not see ministry as a hierarchy. The geometry of the Christian ministry is circular, not pyramidal. Each segment of the circle is equal to, and equidistant from, every other section. No one segment of a circle is any closer than any other. A circle has no top or bottom, no beginning or end.

We have tended to think of the institutional Church as a pyramid, with the clergy occupying the apex and the laity at the bottom, rather than as a circle in which all members are equal and equally close to the center. For the Church truly to become the strong, vibrant body of Christ in the world, fully conscious of its mission in and to the world, we will have to forget about hierarchies and consider ministry in terms of focus, sphere, and function. As Boff expressed it in *Church: Charism and Power:*

> We must first recognize that the activity of the laity is not an extension of the hierarchy. He or she is a member of the Church in the secular world and has a direct mandate from Jesus Christ. . . . The laity are exercising a right and a duty when they unite, mobilize, march and initiate movements for action, peace, and justice. The laity do not need the backing of their bishop or pastor for their movement to have a "Christian character." These movements have a Christian character because the laity are true members of the Church, and with their dignity as lay people they act in their own milieu, the world.[14]

Some members of the Church's ordained leadership would gladly encourage the laity to regain their proper place in the body of Christ and would like to see them function in society as they ought. One of them is Archbishop Edward W. Scott, recently retired primate of the Anglican Church in Canada. He recounts the following:

> When I appeared recently before the National Energy Board of Canada, some of the laity suggested I should not have done this to "represent the Church," for they were there already and were themselves "the Church." I agreed.[15]

And so might we.

. . . AND THE CHURCH'S SUPPORTING MINISTERS

For Christ's body the Church to function as a healthy, robust, unified organism with all its parts operating smoothly and to capacity, with its life-blood reaching every cell; for the Church to be a strong body of Christians well equipped to live the "good news" of the Gospel in their lives and to bring its healing, transforming, and prophetic message to the world—it is crucial that its clergy be the men and women best suited to support, affirm, and encourage the ministries of the laity of the body.

The varieties of ministries of the body of Christ are matters of focus, sphere, and function. The focus of all ministry is the world for which Christ lived and died; every other aspect of ministry must be considered in its light. The Church exists not for and of itself but for the world; the primary ministry of the body, therefore, is not among its own members but in the world. Fundamentally, the ministerial sphere of the ordained members of the body is the Church, whereas that of lay members of the body is the world. The ministry of the laity, because of its focus in the world, is *the* primary ministry of the Church.

Clerical ministries are far easier to define and describe because they are confined within the institutional Church. The ministry of laypersons is far more complex because it is literally as wide as the world. In addition to being active in the world, laypersons at the same time have responsibilities as congregational members. The clergy have both feet, as it were, planted in the institutional Church; laypersons have one foot in the world and the other in the Church, for though service to the world is of primary importance to them, they also participate in the organizational life of the Church. As parishioners, laity function in at least two basic ways: (1) they assume responsibility for the life and maintenance of the community of the faithful according to their gifts and the needs of the community, and (2) they bring to the community the world's concerns, fears, and aspirations, which they then offer to the action of the Eucharist.

Because of the complex and often confusing nature of lay ministries, it is crucial that the clergy see their function as that of providing the unity, the encouragement, the example of loving service to Christ for the laity to emulate in their worldly sphere. Clerical ministries ought to be understood as supportive of all the other ministries of the body. Gutiérrez explains:

> The priest breaks off at the point of his insertion into the world.
> His mission is identified with that of the Church: to evangelize and
> to inspire the temporal order. . . . The layman's position in the

Church, on the other hand, does not require him to abandon his insertion in the world. It is his responsibility to *build up both the Church and the world.* [16]

To do so the laity have the right to expect the clergy to fulfill their main function—that of supporting the former's ministries.

We generally regard support the other way around, in terms of the laity supporting the Church (and, by implication, its clergy). We often hear the clergy lament that "the laity don't support the Church." But the evidence is far more weighted in the other direction. The clergy, by and large, have not learned to support the lay ministries in appropriate ways, nor have they fully appreciated that the laity are just as much the Church as they.

If the Church is to be understood in the organic sense as the body of Christ, it follows that the ministry of the ordained has to be reformed along with that of the laity. The need for such a major overhaul has been amply covered by such eminent Roman Catholic theologians as Hans Küng, Leonardo Boff, and Edward Schillebeeckx. [17]

Roman Catholic leaders have by no means been alone in expressing the urgent need for reform. The authors of an Episcopal Church-commissioned consultation on ordained ministries (1982) called for drastic reform:

> We found that what is necessary is nothing less than a radical shift in the current ideology of priesthood. [18]

After remarking on the inappropriateness of calling presbyters "priests" and suggesting that we revive the former term, the report goes on to explain:

> If the heart of the ordained ministry is pastoral leadership, it follows that a presbyter is to be ordained when there is a community which calls or accepts that person as such. Nothing could be farther from the deep instincts of the Christian tradition than the modern notion that one's vocation to the presbyterate is a matter only between the one so called and God (or that ordination is an ecclesiastical award, a measure of "true" Christian commitment, or an elevation to a higher status).

> Hand in hand with the central role of the community goes the corollary that just as the entire community is a gathering of ministers serving one another and the world, so the ordained ministry is one of service. The ordered ministry is to serve the laity, not vice-versa. [19]

If one considers Christ's Church in the Pauline metaphor, as an organic body in which each member functions in relationship to all the others and that it is a body in distinct relationship to its environment, then we will be given clues to who should be the clergy and how they should be selected. The clergy in a reformed Church would be the natural leaders to emerge from the life and ministry of each congregation. They would be easily identifiable because they would be those who are trusted and respected, mature people who have demonstrated their native gifts for leadership. They would be big-hearted, loving people whose reliability had stood the test of time. Unquestionably, some persons of this description already serve as ordained ministers, but the Church is crying out for many more of them.

The kind of person just described would probably have little difficulty accepting and living out the role as the ordained leader in the priestly community that called him or her into ordained service. He or she ought to be able fully, confidently, and competently to support the ministries of the community's lay members. For this to happen, the ordained person must arise from the congregation of which he or she is a part. And, of course, that person's ordained ministry would be understood only in relationship to the community that called him or her into service, for we know that just because a person happens to be a leader in one place, his or her leadership is not necessarily transferable to another. Thus, with the possible exception of bishops, there would be no more absolute ordinations.

Two of the best descriptions of what the ordained ministry could be come from the foreign mission field. One writing in the 1920s and the other in 1976, both present a very Pauline style of ministry.

Roland Allen was an opinionated and sometimes cantankerous Anglican. He wrote about the ordained ministry from the perspective of his experiences in China (before the Boxer Rebellion), Western Canada, and Africa. His views were neither appreciated nor accepted by his British colleagues, but now, many in the Church who are concerned with the state of the ordained ministry are beginning to pay belated attention to them. Allen wrote:

> A parish priest ought to be a leader of his people, and we are very unready to learn the truth that we cannot create leaders in divinity schools. Anyone who has been in the mission field will recognize the portrait [of the person who ought to be ordained]. The man lives before our eyes. He is a man of mature age, the head of a family. His household [is] well governed and orderly. He is a man of some position in the community. Strangers and visitors on their

journeys are naturally directed to his house, and he knows how to entertain them and can do so. He is a man of certain gravity and dignity whose words carry weight. He can teach and rebuke those who would slight the exhortations of lesser men. He is a man of moral character: he can attend a feast without getting drunk; he can control his temper; he can rule without violence. . . . He is sober-minded and just: he can settle disputes with a judgment which men respect. He is a Christian of some standing. He has learned the teaching of the Apostles and he holds it fast. He can teach what he has learned.[20]

His picture of the presbyter is one of natural leadership that has emerged from a particular community (a community wider than the more narrowly defined religious community).

Leadership cannot be made or manufactured. Some persons are leaders of their peers and others are not. Leaders can be taught to be more effective, but we cannot make them where distinct talents for leadership are not already present, just as we cannot make writers and artists. The same applies to the ordained leaders of Christian communities. Academic knowledge can be taught—indeed, every presbyter needs thorough training, much of it academic—but no amount of seminary training will make the leaders the Church needs (in fact, it would be wrong to expect it to). Given fundamental intelligence, other factors are more important for the ordained leaders in the community of Jesus Christ than intellectual training.

Writing out of his experience among the Masai in East Africa, Vincent J. Donovan presents another cameo of what Christian community and its natural leadership might be:

That man who called the community together; at the end of the instructions he would not be the one in the community who knew the most theology, the theologian. He would not be the preacher or the evangelist of the community. He would not be the prophet. He would not be the most important member of the community. But he could be the focal point of the whole community, the one who would enable the community to act, whether in worship or in service. He would be the animator of the individual members of the community, enabling them to make their various contributions, enabling the preacher to preach and the teacher to teach and the prayer to pray and the prophet to prophesy. He would be the necessary sign of the power that is in all of them. He would be the sign of the unity that exists among them. He would be the link with the outside, the sign of union with the universal Church. He would be their priest.

And he would not be painted into a sacramental corner or restricted to the sacristy. Wherever and whenever the community acted as Christian community he would be carrying out his function, the focal point of the whole community, building that community, holding it together, animating it to action, signifying its unity, enabling it to function. If that community were at worship in the liturgy of the Word, he would not be the reader or the preacher or the teacher; he would be the one enabling those people, not as individuals, but as a community, to hear that Word, to understand it, to judge it and discern it, to make it live, to let it act on them.[21]

Finally, if we truly believe, as did Martin Luther, that the presbyter does what, in principle, every other Christian can do, then we should consider that laypersons, at times, ought to be allowed to preside at the Eucharist. As it is, laypersons can hear confessions and, if necessary baptize. The Church has been loathe to extend its permission to pronouncing of the absolution and presiding at the Eucharist, although there is no biblical or theological reason why it should not.

Presidency at the Eucharist ought to be in the same class as baptism: to be presided over in cases of necessity. If one considers the Christian community an organic body and if we recall that its Eucharist is patterned after the ancient Jewish family meal, then we ought to regard lay presidency as a reasonable proposal. I see it occurring when the presbyter is away from his or her congregation; another leader in the congregation—a layperson—could then preside. In this respect, the Eucharist ought to be thought of as another family meal. Each family meal is at once both very special and very ordinary. A "guest housewife" doesn't customarily preside at the family meal. When I am away from my family another member presides over the dinner table; the family does not send out for a supply, or interim, housewife and mother to "take the meal." Supply priests, communion from the reserved sacrament, or perhaps no celebration of the Eucharist at all—none would be necessary if the Church were to permit lay presidency. The Eucharistic celebration of the community of the faithful is of the utmost importance. It should never be omitted for lack of an ordained leader.

A renewed ministry such as that described by Allen and Donovan, a greater sharing of priestly ministry within the body (lay presidency being just one example), *is* possible. It requires a recovered and renewed appreciation of the whole Church as the organic body of Christ, a community of the faithful in which all members generously share themselves and their gifts for the work of ministry, as St. Paul so elegantly expressed it:

There is one body and one Spirit, just as you are called to the one hope that belongs to your call, one Lord, one faith, one baptism, one God and Father of us all, who is above all and through all and in all. But grace was given to each of us according to the measure of Christ's gift. And his gifts were that some should be apostles, some prophets, some evangelists, some pastors and teachers, to equip the saints for the work of ministry, for building up the body of Christ, until we all attain to the unity of the faith and of the knowledge of the Son of God, to maturity, to the measure of the stature of the fullness of Christ. . . . We are to grow up in every way into him who is the head, into Christ, from whom the whole body, joined and knit together by every joint with which it is supplied, when each part is working properly, makes bodily growth and upbuilds itself in love [Ephesians 4:4–7, 11–16].

A LIBERATED CHURCH

If Christ's Church is to be thoroughly and genuinely reformed, nothing less than a radical recovery of the New Testament idea of the priesthood of the Church and nothing more than imagination and God's magnificent grace will be required. Only in such a Church—liberated to be itself—will the goals of the Gospel be fully accomplished.

Yes, these dry bones can live, if . . .

NOTES AND REFERENCES

INTRODUCTION

1. Edward Schillebeeckx, *Ministry: Leadership in the Community of Jesus Christ* (New York: Crossroad, 1984), p. 142.

CHAPTER 1: THE MINISTERS OF THE CHURCH

1. Leonardo Boff, *Jesus Christ Liberator: A Critical Christology for Our Time* (Maryknoll, NY: Orbis Books, 1978), pp. 248, 250, 252.
2. "A Chicago Declaration of Christian Concern," (n.p., December 1977).
3. *The Book of Common Prayer,* p. 855.
4. Hans Küng, *The Church,* (Garden City, NY: Doubleday and Company, 1976), p. 466.
5. Gregory XVI in Leonardo Boff, *Church: Charism and Power,* trans. John W. Diercksmeir (London: SCM Press, 1985), p. 142.
6. Piux X *Vehementer,* in Juan Luis Segundo, *The Sacraments Today,* trans. John Drury (Maryknoll, NY: Orbis Books, 1974), p. 57.
7. Mark Gibbs, "The Laity and the Institutional Churches," Audenshaw Documents, no. 71, Laity Basics no. 4 (Mucker, Richmond, N. Yorkshire, England: Audenshaw Foundation, March 1977), p. 2.
8. Durstan McDonald et al., "Towards a Theology of Priesthood," Report of the Council for the Development of Ministry and the Board for Theological Education of the Episcopal Church, Trinity Institute, January 1982, pp. 2, 7.
9. Editorial, "For Clergy, Read Laity," *Clergy Review* (February, 1977), p. 43.
10. Richard Broholm, "The Call to Ministry in the Workplace: The Unfinished Reformation Agenda," (unpublished paper, n.d.), p. 48.

CHAPTER 2: THE PRIESTHOOD OF THE CHURCH

1. Robert W. Hovda, *Strong, Loving and Wise: Presiding in Liturgy* (Washington, DC: The Liturgical Conference, 1976), p. 2.

2. Vincent J. Donovan, *Christianity Rediscovered: An Epistle from the Masai* (Notre Dame, IN: Fides/Claretian, 1976), p. 140.

3. Hans Küng, *The Church,* (Garden City, NY: Doubleday and Company, 1976), p. 487.

4. Oscar Cullmann, *Early Christian Worship,* trans. A. Stewart Todd and James B. Torrance (London: SCM Press, 1953), pp. 10-11.

5. Hippolytus, in Henry Chadwick, *The Early Church* (Middlesex, England: Penguin Books, 1967), p. 264.

6. Wayne A. Meeks, *The First Urban Christians: The Social World of the Apostle Paul* (New Haven: Yale University Press, 1983), p. 134.

7. Ibid., p. 111.

8. Edward Schillebeeckx, *Ministry: Leadership in the Community of Jesus Christ* (New York: Crossroad, 1984), pp. 49, 139.

9. Ibid., pp. 38-39, 53.

10. Hans Küng, *Signposts for the Future* (Garden City, NY: Doubleday and Company, 1978), p. 134.

11. A. Theodore Eastman, *The Baptizing Community: Christian Initiation and the Local Congregation* (Wilton, CT: Morehouse Publishing, 1990), p. 61.

12. Aidan Kavanagh, in Durstan R. McDonald, "Towards a Theology of Priesthood," Report of the Council of the Development of Ministry, *The Blue Book: Reports of the Committees, Commissions, Boards and Agencies of the General Convention of the Episcopal Church* (New Orleans, September 1982), p. 193.

13. Küng, *The Church,* pp. 466-67.

14. Durstan R. McDonald et al., "Towards a Theology of Priesthood," Trinity Institute, January 1982, p. 2.

15. Ronald C. D. Jasper and Geoffrey Cuming, *Prayers of the Eucharist: Early and Reformed,* 2d ed. (New York: Oxford University Press, 1980), p. 76.

16. *Book of Common Prayer* (Episcopal), p. 308.

17. Schillebeeckx, *Ministry,* p. 48.

18. Michael Green, *Evangelism in the Early Church* (Grand Rapids, MI: Eerdmans Publishing Co., 1970), p. 274. *See also:* Roland Allen, *The Spontaneous Expansion of the Church* (Grand Rapids, MI: Eerdmans Publishing Co., 1982).

19. Jürgen Moltmann, *The Power of the Powerless* (San Francisco: Harper and Row, 1983), p. 159.

20. Aristides, "Apology," in H.L. Milne, "A New Fragment of the Apology of Aristides," *Journal of Theological Studies* 25 (1924): 216-18.

21. "Letter to Diognetus," in *Early Christian Fathers,* vol. 1, ed. Cyril C. Richardson (Philadelphia: Westminster Press, 1953), pp. 216-18.

22. Küng, *The Church,* p. 489.

23. Robert Murray, "Christianity's 'Yes' to Priesthood," in *The Christian Priesthood,* ed. Nicholas Lash and Joseph Rhymer (London: Darton, Longman and Todd, 1970), p. 38.

CHAPTER 3: THE LIBERATION OF THE LAITY

1. Gustavo Gutiérrez, *A Theology of Liberation,* ed. and trans. Caridad Inda and John Eagleson (Maryknoll, NY: Orbis Books, 1973), pp. 192-93.

2. Robert Hovda, *Strong, Loving and Wise: Presiding in Liturgy* (Washington, DC: The Liturgical Conference, 1976), p. 5.

3. Gutiérrez, *Theology of Liberation,* p. 177.

4. Paulo Freire, *Pedagogy of the Oppressed,* trans. Myra B. Ramos (New York: Herder and Herder), pp. 31-32.

5. Ibid., p. 32.

6. Henri J.M. Nouwen, *Gracias* (San Francisco: Harper and Row, 1983), p. 19.

7. Gutiérrez, *Theology of Liberation,* p. 143.

8. Robert Escarpit, *Ecole Laique, Ecole Du Peuple* (Paris: Calman-Lévy, 1961), p. 43.

CHAPTER 4: THE CLERICAL CAPTIVITY OF THE CHURCH

1. Henry Chadwick, *The Early Church* (Middlesex, England: Penguin Books, 1967), p. 62.

2. Adolf Von Harnack, *Mission and the Expansion of Christianity in the First Three Centuries,* 2 vols., 2d ed., trans. and ed. James Moffatt (New York: Putnam, 1908), p. 368.

3. Michael Green, *Evangelism in the Early Church* (Grand Rapids, MI: Eerdmans Publishing Co., 1970), pp. 172, 175.

4. Arnold Toynbee, *An Historian's Approach to Religion,* quoted in George H. Williams, "The Ancient Church," *The Layman in Christian History,* ed. Stephen Neill and Hans-Rudi Weber (Philadelphia: Westminster Press, 1963), p. 51.

5. Henry Chadwick, *The Early Church,* p. 164.

6. James MacKinnon, *From Christ to Constantine* (New York: Longmans, Green and Co., 1936), pp. 539, 552.

7. J. Vogt, *The Decline of Rome: The Metamorphosis of Ancient Civilization* (New York: Praeger, 1956), p. 94.

8. Jürgen Moltmann, *The Power of the Powerless* (San Francisco: Harper and Row, 1983), p. 158.

9. MacKinnon, *From Christ to Constantine,* p. 551.

10. Mark Sheridan, "The Origins of Monasticism in the Eastern Church," *The Rule of St. Benedict—1980,* ed. Timothy Fry et al. (Collegeville, MN: The Liturgical Press, 1981), p. 16.

11. MacKinnon, *From Christ to Constantine,* p. 551.

12. Owen Chadwick, ed., *Western Ascetism* (Philadelphia: Westminster Press, 1958), p. 14.

13. MacKinnon, *From Christ to Constantine,* pp. 418-19.

14. Mark Sheridan, "The Origins of Monasticism," pp. 14–15.

15. Owen Chadwick, *Western Ascetism,* p. 20.

16. Ibid., p. 23.

17. Ibid., p. 21.

18. Jean Leclercq, "The Priesthood in the Patristic and Medieval Church," in *The Christian Priesthood,* ed. Nicholas Lash and Joseph Rhymer (Denville, NJ: Dimension Books, 1970), p. 54.

19. R. W. Southern, "The Church of the Dark Ages," in *The Layman in Christian History,* ed. by Stephen C. Neill and Hans-Rudi Weber (Philadelphia: Westminster Press, 1963), p. 103.

20. Edward Schillebeeckx, *Ministry: Leadership in the Community of Jesus Christ* (New York: Crossroad, 1984), p. 55.

21. Hubert Jedin, *Ecumenical Councils of the Catholic Church* (Edinburgh and London: Nelson, 1960), p. 71.

22. Roland H. Bainton, "The Ministry in the Middle Ages," in *The Ministry in Historical Perspectives,* ed. H. Richard Niebuhr and Daniel D. Williams (New York: Harper and Brothers, 1956), pp. 90-91.

23. Ibid., p. 91.

24. Martin Luther, "The Babylonian Captivity of the Church," *Three Treatises* (Philadelphia: Muhlenberg Press, 1960), p. 142.

25. Tissa Balasuriya, *The Eucharist and Human Liberation* (Maryknoll, NY: Orbis Books, 1979), pp. 29-30.

26. John T. McNeill, *A History of the Cure of Souls* (New York: Harper and Brothers, 1951), p. 112.

27. Ibid., p. 149.

28. Quoted in Jean Leclercq, "The Priesthood in the Patristic and Medieval Church," p. 66.

29. Ibid., p. 67.

30. Ibid., p. 73.

31. Christopher N.L. Brooke, "The Church of the Middle Ages," in *The Layman in Christian History,* p. 118.

32. Ibid., p. 118.

33. Hans Küng, *The Church,* (Garden City, NY: Doubleday and Company, 1976), pp. 322-23.

34. Claude Peifer, "The Rule of St. Benedict," in *The Rule of St. Benedict* (Collegeville, MN: The Liturgical Press, 1981), p. 65.

35. Roland H. Bainton, "The Ministry in the Middle Ages," in *The Ministry in Historical Perspectives,* p. 95.

36. Christopher N.L. Brooke, "The Church in the Middle Ages," p. 120.

37. Jan Grootaers, "The Roman Catholic Church, *The Layman in Christian History,* p. 299.

38. Martin Luther, Dietrich Steinwede, quoted in *Reformation* (Philadelphia: Fortress Press, 1983), p. 16.

39. Martin Luther, "An Open Letter to the Christian Nobility of the German Nation Concerning the Reform of the Christian Estate" (1520), in *Three Treatises: Martin Luther,* ed. Board of Publications of the United Lutheran Church in America (Philadelphia: Muhlenberg Press, 1960), p. 14.

40. Ibid., pp. 14–15.

41. Ibid., p. 15.

42. Ibid., p. 16. Also: Hubert Jedin, *Ecumenical Councils of the Catholic Church,* pp. 161-64.

43. E. Gordon Rupp, "The Age of the Reformation, 1500-1648," *The Layman in Christian History,* p. 139.

44. Ibid., p. 139.

45. Martin Luther, "The Babylonian Captivity of the Church," in *Three Treatises: Martin Luther,* ed. Board of Publications of the United Lutheran Church in America, (Philadelphia: Muhlenberg Press, 1960), pp. 136, 142.

46. Roland H. Bainton, *Here I Stand: A Life of Martin Luther,* (New York: New American Library, 1950), p. 272.

47. Ibid., p. 272.

48. Ibid., p. 254, and E. Gordon Rupp, "The Age of Reformation," p. 44.

49. Dietrich Steinwede, *Reformation,* p. 44.

50. Ibid., p. 46.

51. Ibid., p. 46.

52. Prayers of the People, Form II, (Episcopal) *Book of Common Prayer* (New York: Church Hymnal Corporation, 1979), p. 385.

53. John Macquarrie, *The Faith of the People of God: A Lay Theology* (New York: Charles Scribner's Sons, 1972), p. 140.

54. Howard Grimes, "The United States, 1800-1962," in *The Layman in Christian History,* p. 240.

55. William W. Sweet, *Religion on the American Frontier,* vol. 1 *Baptists, 1783-1830* (New York: Henry Holt and Company, 1931), p. 36.

56. Hendrik Kraemer, *A Theology of the Laity* (London: Lutterworth Press, 1958), p. 30.

57. Anne W. Rowthorn, "A History of the Evolution and Development of Therapeutic Recreation Services for Special Populations in the United States from 1918 to the Present" (Ph.D. diss., New York University, 1977), pp. 20-21.

58. Ibid., pp. 18-22.

59. Hans-Rudi Weber, "The Rediscovery of the Laity in the Ecumenical Movement," in *The Layman in Christian History,* p. 378.

60. W.A. Visser 't Hooft and J.H. Oldham, *The Church and Its Function in Society* (London: Allen and Unwin, 1937), pp. 117–18.

61. Hans-Rudi Weber, "The Rediscovery of the Laity in the Ecumenical Movement," in *The Layman in Christian History,* p. 378.

62. Jan Grootaers, "The Roman Catholic Church," *The Layman in Christian History,* p. 335.

CHAPTER 5: THE THEOLOGY OF THE LAITY BY THE LAITY

1. John Macquarrie, *The Faith of the People of God* (New York: Charles Scribner's Sons, 1972), pp. 162-63.

2. Gustavo Gutiérrez, *We Drink from Our Own Wells: The Spiritual Journey of a People,* trans. Matthew J. O'Connell (Maryknoll, NY: Orbis Books, 1984), p. 1.

3. Francisco José Moreno, *Between Faith and Reason,* (New York: Harper and Row, 1977), p. 88.

4. Richard Mouw, "Understanding the Mission of the American Laity," *Laity Exchange* (1978), pp. 3-4.

5. Barnett Newmann, museum notes to "The Stations of the Cross," a series painted from 1958-1966, on display at the National Gallery of Art, Washington, D.C.

6. John Macquarrie, *The Faith of the People of God,* p. 17.

7. Ibid., pp. 22-23.

8. Richard Mouw, "Understanding the Mission of the American Laity," p. 4.

9. Ibid., p. 4.

10. Kairos Theologians, *The Kairos Document: Challenge to the Church: A Theological Comment on the Political Crisis in South Africa* (Braamfontein, South Africa: Springs Advertiser, 1985), p. i.

11. Ibid., p. 26.

12. Leonardo Boff, *Way of the Cross—Way of Justice,* trans. John Drury (Maryknoll, NY: Orbis Books, 1980), p. vii.

CHAPTER 6: FOLLOWING JESUS

1. Katherine Dyckman and L. Patrick Carroll, *Inviting the Mystic, Supporting the Prophet* (New York: Paulist Press, 1981), p. 79.

2. Gustavo Gutiérrez, *We Drink from Our Own Wells: The Spiritual Journey of a People,* trans. Matthew J. O'Connell (Maryknoll, NY: Orbis Books, 1984), pp. 4, 89.

3. Ibid., p. 88.

4. Dietrich Bonhoeffer, *Letters and Papers from Prison,* trans. Reginald H. Fuller, ed. Eberhard Bethge (New York: Macmillan Co., 1962), p. 222.

5. Ibid., pp. 222-23.
6. Maryknoll Society, quoted in Henri J. M. Nouwen, *Gracias: A Latin American Journal* (San Francisco: Harper and Row, 1983), p. 6.
7. Louis Weil, *Sacraments and Liturgy: The Outward Signs* (Oxford: Basil Blackwell Publisher, 1983), pp. 91–92.
8. Ibid., p. 91.
9. Gutiérrez, *We Drink from Our Own Wells,* p. 15.
10. Ibid., p. 16.
11. Leonard Doohan, *The Lay-Centered Church: Theology and Spirituality* (Minneapolis, MN: Winston Press, 1984), p. 42.
12. Gutiérrez, *We Drink from Our Own Wells,* p. 14.
13. W. H. Auden, "Foreword," in Dag Hammarskjöld, *Markings,* trans. and ed. Leif Sjoberg and W. H. Auden (New York: Alfred A. Knopf, 1966), p. xxi.
14. Leonardo Boff, *Way of the Cross—Way of Justice,* trans. John Drury (Maryknoll, NY: Orbis Books, 1982), p. 48.
15. E. B. Pusey, "God With Us," *Parochial Sermons,* vol. 1 (Oxford, 1852), pp. 58-59.
16. Dag Hammarskjöld, *Markings,* p. 122.
17. Edward Schillebeeckx, *The Church with a Human Face: A New and Expanded Theology of Ministry* (London: SCM Press, 1985), pp. 190, 195-97.
18. Ibid., p. 197.
19. Ibid., p. 190.
20. John A. T. Robinson, *Honest to God* (London: SCM Press, 1963), p. 94.
21. Eleanor L. McLaughlin, "Priestly Spirituality," *Anglican Theological Review,* 1981; reprinted by Ascension Press, Philadelphia, n.d., p. 18.
22. Leonardo Boff, *Way of the Cross—Way of Justice,* trans. John Drury (Maryknoll, NY: Orbis Books, 1980), p. 46.

CHAPTER 7: RUNNING WITH THE SAINTS

1. Francis W. Johnston, *Heart of the Saints: The Christian Ideal in the Lives and Ecumenical Teaching of the Saints* (London: T. Snand, 1975), p. 17.
2. Leonard Doohan, *The Lay-Centered Church: Theology and Spirituality* (Minneapolis, MN: Winston Press, 1984), p. 43.
3. Ibid., p. 43.
4. Statistics from: Standing Liturgical Commission of The Episcopal Church, *Lesser Feasts and Fasts,* 3d ed. (New York: Church Hymnal Corporation, 1980).
5. "New Names for Calendar," *The Living Church* 190 (14 April, 1985): 6.
6. Statistics from *The Lutheran Book of Worship,* 1978.
7. Leonard Doohan, *The Lay-Centered Church,* pp. 42–43.
8. Carl Sandburg, introduction to *Lincoln's Devotional* (Great Neck, NY: Channel Press, 1957), p. viii.
9. Abraham Lincoln, quoted in introduction to *Lincoln's Devotional,* p. xiii.
10. Dorothy Day, *The Long Loneliness: The Autobiography of Dorothy Day* (New York: Harper and Brothers, 1952), pp. 33, 39, 42, 45.
11. Ibid., p. 204.
12. W. H. Auden, foreword to *Markings,* p. xx.
13. Dag Hammarskjöld, *Markings,* p. 5.
14. Ibid., p. 205.
15. Ibid., p. 154.
16. Ibid., p. 165.
17. Ibid., p. 214.

18. Juan Luis Segundo, *The Sacraments Today,* trans. John Drury (Maryknoll, NY: Orbis Books, 1974), p. 14.

19. Cesar Chavez, in Jacquez E. Levy, *Cesar Chavez: Autobiography of La Causa* (New York: Norton and Co., 1975), p. 161.

20. Ibid., p. 227.

21. Ibid., p. 242.

22. Ibid., p. 286.

23. Ibid., p. 465.

24. Jürgen Moltmann, *The Power of the Powerless* (San Francisco: Harper and Row, 1983), p. 120.

25. From the dedication of this book.

26. Leonardo Boff, *Jesus Christ Liberator,* p. 220.

27. Alfons Auer, *Open to the World: An Analysis of Lay Spirituality* (Baltimore: Helicon Press, 1966), pp. 334-35.

28. William Stringfellow, *My People is the Enemy: An Autobiographical Polemic* (New York: Holt, Rinehart and Winston, 1964), p. 129.

29. Jim Wallis, "A Tribute to William Stringfellow," *Sojourners* (April 1985): 2.

30. Ibid.

31. Leonardo Boff, *Way of the Cross—Way of Justice,* trans. John Drury (Maryknoll, NY: Orbis Books, 1980), p. 40.

32. Jacob Epstein, in Basil Spence, *Phoenix at Coventry: The Building of a Cathedral* (New York: Harper and Row, 1962), p. 70.

33. C. Wright Mills, "On Intellectual Craftsmanship," *The Sociological Imagination* (New York: Oxford University Press, 1959), p. 196.

34. Leonardo Boff, *Jesus Christ Liberator,* p. 219.

35. Theobald H. Schenck, hymn 130, *The Hymnal of the Protestant Episcopal Church in the United States of America, 1940* (New York: Church Hymnal Corporation, 1940).

CHAPTER 8: KEEPING STABLE THE FABRIC OF THE WORLD

1. George Peck, "Reconceiving the Ministry of the Laity: A Personal Testimony," *The 99 Percenter,* n.s., no. 5 (September 1982): 1–2.

2. Ibid., p. 1.

3. Roland Allen, "Voluntary Clergy," in *The Compulsion of the Spirit,* ed. David Paton and Charles H. Long (Grand Rapids: William B. Eerdmans, 1983), pp. 104-5. [The quotation was originally published in 1930 in Allen's book *The Case for Voluntary Clergy.*]

4. Cynthia Wedel, "A Response," to "Decree on the Apostolate of the Laity," *Documents of Vatican II,* ed. Walter M. Abbott, trans. Joseph Gallagher, (New York: America Press, 1966), p. 522.

5. "Evangelization in Latin America's Present and Future, Report of 3rd General Conference of the Latin American Episcopate, Puebla de Los Angeles, Mexico, January 27-February 13, 1979, #789, 795–98, in *Puebla and Beyond,* ed. John Eagleson and Philip Scharper, trans. John Drury (Maryknoll, NY: Orbis Books, 1979), pp. 229-30.

6. "God's People in Ministry," A Report to the 1984 Convention of the Lutheran Church in America (Philadelphia: Division of Professional Leadership, 1984), p. 16.

7. *Puebla Document,* #811 and 815, p. 231.

8. John A. T. Robinson, *Honest to God* (London: SCM Press, 1963), pp. 100–101.

9. Oscar Romero, *The Church is All of You: Thoughts of Archbishop Oscar Romero* (London: William Collins and Sons, 1985), p. 117.

10. Gustavo Gutiérrez, *We Drink from Our Own Wells: The Spiritual Journey of a People,* trans. Matthew J. O'Connell (Maryknoll, NY: Orbis Books, 1984), p. 37.

11. "Giving Mission Its Proper Place," Report of the Mission Issues and Strategy Group of the Anglican Consultative Council, 1984, p. 6.

CHAPTER 9: WHERE JESUS WANTS TO BE FOLLOWED

1. Leonardo Boff, *Jesus Christ Liberator,* trans. Patrick Hughes (Maryknoll, NY: Orbis Books, 1978), p. 220.

2. Charles Gore et al., *Property: Its Duties and Rights* (London: Macmillan Co., 1915), pp. xix-xx.

3. Gustavo Gutiérrez, *A Theology of Liberation,* trans. and ed. Caridad Inda and John Eagleson (Maryknoll, NY: Orbis Books, 1973), p. 291.

4. "La Pobreza de la Iglesia," Documento #14, *Medellin: Reflexiones en el CELAM* (Madrid: Biblioteca de Autores Cristianos, 1977), pp. 184-85. ("Poverty of the Church," Latin American Episcopal Council.)

5. David B. Barrett, ed., *World Christian Encyclopedia: A Comprehensive Study of Churches and Religions in the Modern World* (Nairobi and New York: Oxford University Press, 1982), global map #2, "Growth of Organized Christianity, 1980," p. 865.

6. David B. Barrett, *World Christian Encyclopedia,* global map #4, p. 866.

7. David B. Barrett, *World Christian Encyclopedia,* global map #6, p. 867.

8. Leonardo Boff, *Way of the Cross—Way of Justice,* trans. John Drury (Maryknoll, NY: Orbis Books, 1980), pp. 5, 47-48.

9. Note: The word "preferential," in the phrase "preferential option for the poor," is not *exclusive,* because although God *prefers,* he never *excludes* anybody.

10. "Evangelization in Latin America's Present and Future," Conference of the Latin American Episcopate, Puebla de Los Angeles, Mexico, January 27-February 1979, in *Puebla and Beyond,* ed. John Eagleson and Philip Scharper (Maryknoll, NY: Orbis Books, 1979), #1141 and #1142, p. 265.

11. Conrad Noel, *An Autobiography,* ed. Sidney Dark (London: J.M. Dent and Sons, 1945), p. 30.

12. *Didache* #5, in *Early Christian Fathers,* vol. 1, ed. Cyril Richardson (Philadelphia: Westminster Press, 1953), p. 171.

13. Lactantius, quoted in Clive Barrett, *To The Fathers They Shall Go: Wealth and Poverty in Early Christian Thought* (London: Jubilee Group, 1984), p. 18.

14. Note: Refer to *To The Fathers They Shall Go* by Clive Barrett (cited above) for a full treatment of the early Christians' concepts of wealth and poverty.

15. Ambrose, quoted in Clive Barrett, *To The Fathers They Shall Go,* pp. 33-34.

16. Aristides, Ap. XV, Syriac version, quoted in Igino Giordani, *The Social Message of the Early Church Fathers,* trans. Alba I. Zizzamia (Boston: St. Paul Editions, 1977), p. 307.

17. John Chrysostom, homily #6 on 1 Cor., quoted in Clive Barrett, *To The Fathers They Shall Go,* p. 33.

18. Frank Weston, "Our Present Day," in *Report of the Anglo-Catholic Congress* (London, 1923), pp. 185-86.

19. Gutiérrez, *A Theology of Liberation,* pp. 261–62, passim.

20. Ibid., p. 271.

21. Puebla Document, #1140, in *Puebla and Beyond,* p. 264.

CHAPTER 10: DO THIS IN REMEMBRANCE OF ME

1. John A.T. Robinson, *Essays on Being the Church in the World* (London: SCM Press, 1960), p. 59.

2. Louis Weil, *Sacraments and Liturgy: The Outward Signs* (Oxford: Blackwell Publisher, 1983), p. 93.

3. John A.T. Robinson, *Liturgy Coming to Life* (Philadelphia: Westminster Press, 1960), p. 19.

4. Annie Dillard, *Holy and Firm* (New York: Harper and Row, 1977), p. 59.

5. G. A. Studdert Kennedy, *The Word and the Work* (London: Longmans, Green and Co., 1925), p. 72.

6. Tissa Balasuriya, *The Eucharist and Human Liberation* (Maryknoll, NY: Orbis Books, 1979), p. 62.

7. Juan Luis Segundo, *The Sacraments Today,* vol. 4 in *A Theology for Artisans of a New Humanity,* trans, John Drury (Maryknoll, NY: Orbis Books, 1974), p. 55.

8. Louis Weil, *Sacraments and Liturgy.* For a concise discussion of piety turned inward, *see* chapter 11, "Liturgy and Its Social Dimensions," pp. 89-100.

9. Ibid., p. 97.

10. Paul Gibson, "Liturgy and Justice" (Paper presented to Cathedral Deans of the Anglican Church of Canada, 9 January 1985), p. 1.

11. Segundo, *The Sacraments Today,* pp. 38-39.

12. Studdert Kennedy, *The Word and the Work,* pp. 65-66.

13. John A. T. Robinson, *Liturgy Coming to Life,* p. 31.

14. Segundo, *The Sacraments Today,* p. 59.

15. The Standing Commission on Metropolitan Affairs and the Standing Commission on World Mission of the Episcopal Church, a draft for the General Convention *Blue Book* of "A Common Statement," March 13, 1985. Special acknowledgement is given to the primary authors of the document: Marjorie Christie, Jack Woodard and Roland Foster; to some degree, Anne Rowthorn. pp. 2-3 cited here.

16. Ibid., pp. 3-5.

17. Ibid., pp. 5-6.

18. Paul Gibson, "Liturgy and Justice," p. 8.

19. John A.T. Robinson, *Liturgy Coming to Life,* p. 31.

CHAPTER 11: BUILDING UP THE BODY OF CHRIST

1. John A.T. Robinson, *On Being the Church in the World* (London: SCM Press, 1960), p. 62.

2. Gustavo Gutiérrez, *A Theology of Liberation,* trans. Caridad Inda and John Eagleson (Maryknoll, NY: Orbis Books, 1973), p. 255.

3. Dietrich Bonhoeffer, *Letters and Papers from Prison,* ed. Eberhard Bethge and trans. Reginald H. Fuller (New York: Macmillan Co., 1953), p. 239.

4. Gutiérrez, *A Theology of Liberation,* p. 256.

5. Leonidas Proaño, "Cuaresma y conversón," *Signos de lucha y esperanza: Testimonios de la Iglesia en América latina, 1973-1978* (Lima: CEP, 1978), p. 272.

6. "Unknown Sayings of Jesus," quoted in Leonardo Boff, *Church: Charism and Power* (London: SCM Press, 1985), p. 151.

7. Robert Hovda, *Strong, Loving and Wise: Presiding in Liturgy* (Washington, DC: The Liturgical Conference, 1976), p. 57.

8. John A.T. Robinson, *Honest to God* (London: SCM Press, 1963), p. 87.

9. Bonhoeffer, *Letters and Papers from Prison,* p. 239.

10. Paul Reeves, Godfrey Wilson, and Edward Buckle, "The Church's Use of Its Material Resources (Letter to the clergy of the Anglican Diocese of Auckland, 19 June, 1984).

11. Leonardo Boff, *Jesus Christ Liberator,* trans. Patrick Hughes (Maryknoll, NY: Orbis Books, 1978), pp. 248-49.

12. "Evangelization in the Latin American Church: Communion and Participation," #789, *Puebla and Beyond,* ed. John Eagleson and Philip Scharper (Maryknoll, NY: Orbis Books, 1979), p. 229.

13. Gutiérrez, *A Theology of Liberation,* p. 57.

14. Leonardo Boff, *Church: Charism and Power* (London: SCM Press, 1985), p. 30.

15. Edward Scott, "The Laity and the World Council of Churches: Some Personal Reflections," *Audenshaw Papers,* #69, ed. Mark Gibbs and Trevor Beeson, 1979, p. 3.

16. Gutiérrez, *A Theology of Liberation,* p. 57.

17. Note: The following books are particularly relevant to the discussion of ministry reform: Hans Küng, *The Church* (Garden City, NY: Doubleday, 1976); Edward Schillebeeckx: *Ministry: Leadership in the Community of Jesus* (New York: Crossroad, 1984) and *The Church with a Human Face* (London: SCM Press, 1985); and Leonardo Boff, *Church: Charism and Power* (London: SCM Press, 1985).

18. Durstan R. McDonald, "Towards a Theology of Priesthood," Trinity Institute, January 1982, p. 1.

19. Ibid., p. 8.

20. Roland Allen, *Voluntary Clergy* (London: SPCK, 1923), pp. 6-7, 48-49.

21. Vincent J. Donovan, *Christianity Rediscovered* (Notre Dame, IN: Fides/Claretian, 1976), pp. 144-45.

INDEX